HOLY
SPOKES!

A BIKING BIBLE FOR EVERYONE

Rob Coppolillo

To my family for making everything possible, and to Fred Engel for teaching me to write. Most of all, to Rebel, Luca, and Dominic—hey, we did it!

Holy Spokes
A Biking Bible For Everyone
by Rob Collololo

© 2013 Rob Collololo
Illustrations © Todd Telander

First published in 2013 by Zest Books
35 Stillman Street, Suite 121, San Francisco, CA 94107
www.zestbooks.net
Created and produced by Zest Books, San Francisco, CA

Teen Nonfiction / Fitness & Health
Library of Congress Control Number: 2012936086
ISBN: 978-1-936976-23-2

Cover Design: Tanya Napier
Book Design: Marissa Feind, Feind Design
Editor: Daniel Harmon

Manufactured in the U.S.A.
DOC 10 9 8 7 6 5 4 3 2 1
4500394130

HOLY SPOKES!

A BIKING BIBLE FOR EVERYONE

Rob Coppolillo

CONTENTS

FOREWORD

by Dede Barry

Each and every July when I was growing up, I'd be able to stand on the side of the road in front of my house and watch as bike racers flew past me. These cyclists became my heroes; they inspired me. On my first bike, I rode to school, raced friends around the block, and got to really know my hometown of Milwaukee. A few years later, I lined up for my first race (on a borrowed racing bike, which was way too big) on a steaming hot July day. I had on only a pair of plastic sandals, a pair of black shorts, and a white T-shirt. The gun went off, and the rest was a blur of cyclists spinning, sprinting, and flying along the lakefront. After 30 minutes of racing, I bore down on the finish line. I finished second, but the thrill wasn't in the result—it was in the race itself. The party environment, the community surrounding the event, and the effort of the race all had me buzzing: Smoking BBQ pits lined the course, spectators cheered above the MC's thundering voice, and cyclists sped around the circuit. The fans fed my spirit. I was hooked on riding. Slowly, cycling crept into my life and led me on what has become a lifelong and global journey.

As a child, the bike gave me freedom to explore and make new discoveries, and today, decades later, I still feel as though I'm on a unique journey every time I ride. My bike has immersed me in different cultures, cleared my mind, sparked my creativity, carried me over mountain peaks, and exhilarated me on the descents. It's also kept me physically and mentally healthy. I met my husband on my bike, and I've also made many lifelong friends there. We share something, which not only draws us together but also gives us a unique perspective on the world.

When I was a teenager, I moved to Boulder, Colorado (a cycling mecca), to pursue my racing career. While huffing up the foothills of Boulder one sunny winter day, I met Rob Coppolillo. He encouraged me all the way to the top of those hills and then proceeded to entertain me for the duration of the two-hour ride home. We talked about politics, music, school, training, racing, food, wine, European football, Nordic skiing, and even dancing. Rob was an aspiring professional cyclist, but for him, the bike was, and still is, about much more than the finish line. His passion for cycling has always been infectious. Over the years, as we have aged, our friendship has grown. We have both matured, but even now when we ride together I always feel a jovial adolescent freedom that reminds me of the first time we rode together.

Even though my career as a professional cyclist is over now, I still ride almost daily. My bike transports me to and from work, and over to school and the store as well. And I explore the countryside on family bike rides with my children—but for peace and fitness, I escape to the mountains alone. A few hours on the bike invigorates me in a way that nothing else can. For as long as I'm physically able to pedal, my bike will be a source of freedom and exploration. It always takes me where I need to go, and it introduces me to new people and places, and even new ways of thinking—just like it always has.

With his inspirational writing, Rob will introduce you to a sport—and a journey—that has the power to change your life. In the meantime, if you're ever biking around Spain, keep an eye out for me!

Dede Barry was the 1989 junior world champion in road cycling. During her career as a professional, she competed throughout Europe and the United States, winning dozens of races. She was the first American woman to win a World Cup event, and in 2004 she took the silver medal in the time trial at the Athens Olympics. She's married to Michael Barry, also a professional cyclist, and they have two sons, Liam and Ashlin. They live in Girona, Spain.

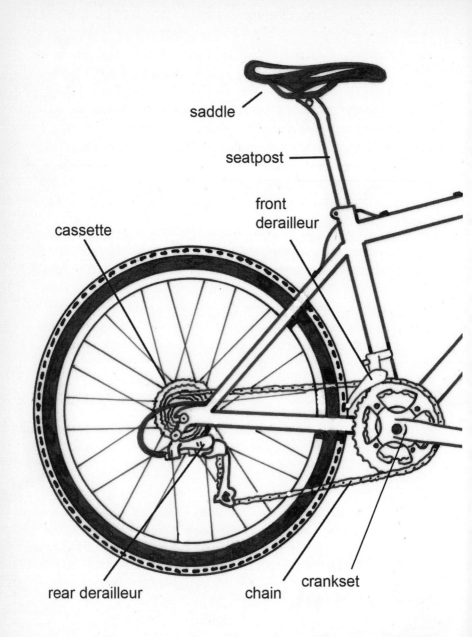

saddle

seatpost

front
derailleur

cassette

rear derailleur

chain

crankset

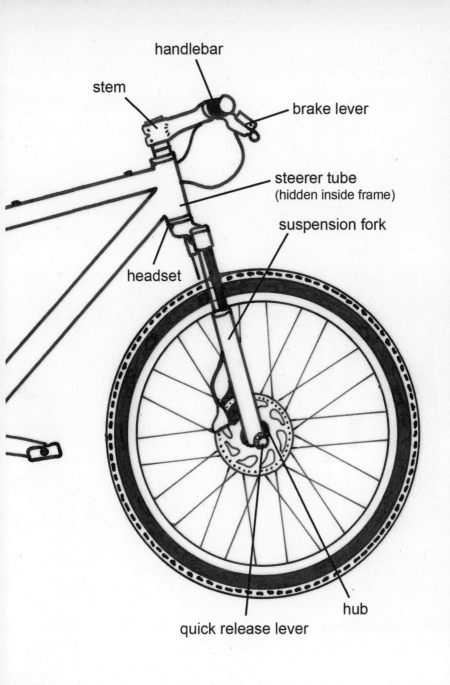

1

A BRIEF HISTORY OF THE BIKE

For many years now most, cycling enthusiasts have attributed the first bicycle design to Leonardo da Vinci, one of the original Renaissance men, at around 1500 CE. Sketches in his Codex Atlanticus show a remarkably modern, two-wheeled machine; the only problem with this picture (so to speak) is that the sketches now appear to be a forgery. A few holdouts like historian Augusto Marinoni still claim Leonardo as the inventor of the bicycle, but whatever the truth of that original design may be, the first modern designs appeared in France and Germany around the 1860s (although there's still a lot of debate about who exactly "invented" the modern machine that we ride today).

Since then, the bike has become a part of everyday life for people around the world. Bikes themselves have evolved into everything from super-light racing machines to utilitarian work vehicles. And that's really the fun of it—because there are so many ways to enjoy cycling today, it appeals to just about everybody.

EUROPEAN RACES AND TWO WORLD WARS

During the 1880s, bicycle design still had a ways to go. Called a vélocipède (or "fast foot"), it had a wooden seat and rims, and some models couldn't even be steered. These bikes lacked pedals, too, so riders just kicked their feet along and held on for the ride. One of these early models was called a "boneshaker" or a "penny farthing." You've probably seen it before—it was the strange-looking contraption with a huge wheel in front and a tiny one in back, with a saddle (seat) placed perilously high in between them. Any guesses why they called it a boneshaker? Ouch!

The boneshakers incorporated pedals into the design, but the pedals were attached directly to the front wheel, much like a little kid's tricycle today. Simple, sure, but it was a primitive design, which overemphasized the front wheel, leaving the ride unstable and dangerous. Riders coined the term "breakneck speed" to describe the results of a high-speed crash on one of these things.

Bone Shaker

By 1885, the "safety bicycle" had replaced the boneshaker. The safety bike looked a lot like what you and I ride today: two wheels of equal size, a saddle perched above the pedals, and handlebars for steering. They were quite a bit easier to ride than the wobbly boneshakers, so folks called them safety bicycles.

It didn't take long for people to start racing one another with their new machinery. The first cycling race probably took place in Europe around 1860, although whether it was the French, Belgians, British, or Germans who hosted the event remains a point of much debate. Wherever it was that the first races took place, they were terribly difficult: The first edition of the Paris to Rouen road race covered 123 kilometers (about seventy-five miles), and the winner arrived after ten hours of "racing"! Modern competitors today might spend two-and-a-half hours on the same course, leaving them time to finish, take a hot bath, have dinner, and catch a nap before their hard-working ancestors would have finished.

These days we take it for granted that women should be able to compete in sports like soccer, basketball, and, yes, cycling. Sadly, however, women were excluded from the early years of bike racing. The earliest events generally didn't include minority groups either, but all this would change as the sport evolved and the modern bicycle became an integral part of life in Europe and the United States.

By 1900, the bike had become an easy, cheap, and reliable transportation option for people all over the world. Bicyclists swarmed the streets of London, Paris, and New York. Racing had become quite a spectator sport, too, with the first edition of the Tour de France gathering great acclaim throughout France in 1903.

Even modern armies adopted the bicycle as a new technology. Soldiers in both World Wars pedaled throughout the battlefields with rifles clipped to their sides and bullets whizzing by. (Imagine that the next time you're late for school and pedaling like mad!)

GROWING PAINS

Bike racing had caught on in the United States, too, with world champions competing in velodrome (track) races at Madison Square Garden and in cities like Denver and Chicago. Many newly arrived European immigrants were familiar with the sport, creating a captive audience. The sport grew in popularity in the late nineteenth and early twentieth century, attracting participants from outside immigrant populations.

Most famous among those was a young black man from Indiana named Marshall "Major" Taylor, who became world champion in the one-mile race in 1899 and 1900, making him the second African American at the time to win a world championship in any sport (boxer George Dixon beat him to the punch, winning the bantamweight world championship in 1890).

Why "Major"?

Taylor earned the nickname "Major" after performing bike tricks in a US military uniform, though he never served in the US military. He found quick success racing on the track, too. He was eventually banned by bigoted race promoters, but found a new racing home in Europe. At one point in 1898, he held seven world records in a variety of distances from the quarter mile to the two mile event, and the velodrome in India-napolis still bears his name to this day.

Renowned for his gentlemanly nature as well as his fast legs, Major Taylor became one of the first African American heroes in American sports.

Taylor and his fellow riders raced in front of raucous crowds throughout the United States. As the sport grew, small towns like Somerville, New Jersey hosted bicycle races of all distances and types. In fact, the Tour of Somerville is the oldest continuously held race in the country, and they've been putting on the event since 1940.

By the 1950s, Americans' sporting tastes had drifted away from cycling and moved toward team sports like baseball, football, and basketball. During the booming economic years after World War II, gasoline was inexpensive and people had the means to buy cars. The bike faded into the background, both as a popular sport and as a practical transportation tool.

THE BIKE MOUNTS A COMEBACK!

An adventurous group of Americans turned the trend around in the 1970s by developing the modern "mountain bike." Military cyclists had tinkered with bikes adapting them to off-road riding, as had a group of French riders in the 1950s, but none of these trends lasted. It took the ingenuity and passion of some Northern California cyclists and innovators to make the idea stick.

During the 1970s, visionaries like Charlie Cunningham, Joe Breeze, Tom Ritchey, and Charlie Kelly took "balloon-tire" bikes, similar to today's "beach cruisers," and outfitted them with derailleurs (the little gadget mounted by the rear wheel that helps change gears). Derailleurs and multiple gears offered easier pedaling uphill, opening new terrain to cyclists. Using fat tires and flat handlebars (instead of curved "road" bars), cyclists began tackling the rolling, forested terrain of Marin County, just north of San Francisco.

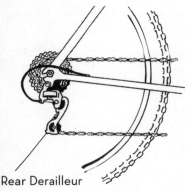

Rear Derailleur

It didn't take long before that same group started racing. On the flanks of Mount Tamalpais, the riders competed in a downhill race known as the "Repack." (After a run, the bikes' drum brakes—an older brake design housed inside a drum or cylinder—would be so fried that they would need to be repacked with grease—hence the name; the trail the race was run on is known by the same name, and riders still flock to it to this day.) Meanwhile, halfway across the United States, another gang had begun riding over Pearl Pass, from Crested Butte to Aspen, in Colorado.

Mountain biking opened up endless miles of off-road terrain. People who loved to hike, backpack, and enjoy nature suddenly had another way to enjoy the outdoors. They could cover twenty miles or more in a day, instead of just a few. Anywhere there was a dirt road or trail, they could ride a bike.

And by this time, cycling wasn't just for men. Jacquie Phelan was an early female cycling pioneer, racing with the guys (and beating plenty of them, too!). She went on to found a counterculture club of free-thinking female riders known as the Women's Mountain Bike and Tea Society (WOMBATS) and represented the United States at the world cycling championships, becoming an icon within the sport. She and her male buddies kick-started the mountain-bike revolution we're still enjoying today.

THE RED ZINGER, THE COORS CLASSIC, AND AMERICAN RACING

In the early 1980s, American cycling received another boost when an enthusiastic kid from Reno, Nevada, took the road scene by storm. Greg LeMond won the junior World Championships in 1979, took silver in the men's World Championships in '82, and finally won it in '83, becoming the first American to do so.

The women weren't far behind. Though many mistakenly believe LeMond to be the first American winner of the Tour de France, it was actually Marianne Martin, a native of Fenton, Michigan. She won the women's Tour in 1984. That same summer, Americans Connie Carpenter Phinney and Rebecca Twigg won the Olympic gold and silver medals respectively in road cycling. By the mid-'80s, American women were at the top of the sport.

The American men did their best to keep pace. LeMond won the Tour de France in 1986, alongside his teammate and fellow American Andy Hampsten, who won "Best Young Rider" from the race organizers. LeMond's story became even more incredible when he narrowly survived a hunting accident in 1987 (his brother-in-law wounded him with a shotgun!), only to return to cycling to win the Tour twice more, in '89 and '90, and another world championship.

The Stage Race: A Race With a Bunch of Races Within It

"Stage races" are days, or even, in the case of the Tour de France, weeks long. Each day, there are two races going on— one for that individual day's "stage" win, and another for the overall prize (usually earned by having the lowest overall time) at the end. The rider who performs the best, day in and day out, wins the overall, while each day's winner is celebrated, but she or he might eventually finish far down on the overall standings.

For example, if day-one riders climb an enormous mountain, and one finishes three hours behind the competition, he could win all the remaining stages (and be celebrated each and every day he wins!), but unless he makes up those three hours that he lost, he won't win the overall. Riders victorious in a three-week race like the "Tour" do everything well and can't afford to have a bad day.

Cycling's popularity boomed. Rising gasoline prices pushed some to return to the bike for transportation. The United States finally had a world-class bike race, too: Sponsored by the Celestial Seasonings tea company from 1975 to 1979, it was known as the "Red Zinger" (one of the company's most popular flavors). In 1980, the Coors Brewing Company threw its support behind the race and built the "Coors Classic" into an international sensation, attracting world champions and crowds numbering in the hundreds of thousands.

The Coors Classic changed its course for each edition of the race, and in 1988, its final year, riders started in Hawaii and concluded in Colorado. After competing in Hawaii, the entire race—staff, riders, and all the equipment—hopped on airplanes and flew to California, where they recommenced the race. Davis Phinney, the first American man to win an individual stage of the Tour de France, won the overall race, which finished in his hometown of Boulder. And incidentally, Phinney's son (with wife and Olympic champion Connie Carpenter Phinney), Taylor, has already won a world championship on the bike, as a junior rider in 2007. And in 2008 and 2012, he represented the United States in the Olympics. Good genes!

LEMOND STARTED THE JOB ARMSTRONG FINISHED

The Coors Classic popularized cycling, especially in Colorado, becoming the state's own Super Bowl. Greg LeMond, Andy Hampsten, Connie Carpenter Phinney, and Inga Thompson became household names to those who grew up near the race. However, while cycling may have been growing in popularity in Colorado, it was still a backwater sport to most of the United States.

Meanwhile, a fiery kid from Texas made headlines in the late '80s as a triathlete. Lance Armstrong won the "Iron Kids" triathlon at thirteen. By the age of eighteen, he'd won a national triathlon championship, competing as a professional. Olympic cycling coaches convinced him to try out for the cycling team, and he spent his senior year of high school at the Olympic Training Center in Colorado Springs. He made the national cycling team and raced at the junior world championships in Russia in 1989. (Dede Barry, author of the foreword to this book, won the junior women's race that year—not a bad team for the Americans.)

Armstrong quickly became one of the best road-cycling pros in the United States. He competed at the Barcelona Olympics in 1992, finishing fourteenth. He moved to a European-based team at the end of that season, and then won the world professional championships in 1993 in Oslo, Norway. By 1996, he was the top-ranked pro in the world— but Lance and cycling still hadn't earned widespread fame in the United States.

Cancer, Seven Tours, and Bikes Galore

After experiencing pain and fatigue on the bike, Armstrong discovered in October of 1996 that he had testicular cancer. Doctors gave him less than a 50-50 chance of living, as the cancer had spread to his lungs and brain. It didn't sound hopeful. The cycling world was stunned.

After surgery and aggressive chemotherapy, his prognosis improved. As his body recovered, his thoughts returned to racing. By the fall of 1998, he had rebuilt himself into an even better cyclist. He placed fourth at the world championships and fourth at the three-week Vuelta a España (or Tour of Spain—that country's version of the Tour de France). Those who were shocked by the illness were even more astounded by his return. He'd beaten cancer at unbelievable odds.

Armstrong returned to the Tour de France in 1999. He'd already defied doctors' expectations by racing again. The '99 Tour transformed him into one of the world's most inspirational figures, particularly to cancer patients and survivors. He began the race with most fans hoping for great things, but no one expecting a victory. He not only won the race, but he also went on to victory in the following six Tours de France, breaking the previous record of five victories in the race. Armstrong was suddenly the most famous sports personality on the planet, better known than Tiger Woods, Michael Jordan, or Cristiano Ronaldo. For good reason—he'd not only overcome advanced testicular cancer, but he'd also returned to one of the most difficult sports events in the world—and he'd won seven consecutive times! During Armstrong's reign as the perennial Tour de France champion, he was consistently in the news—and not just because of his victories. He founded the Lance Armstrong Foundation (LAF)—known for its yellow "Livestrong" bracelets—shortly after his own diagnosis in 1996, and began raising tens of millions of dollars for cancer research, patient support, and education.

Lance Armstrong's Dark Cloud

Lance Armstrong has made headlines for his Tour de France victories, his generous work in cancer awareness and prevention, his celebrity girlfriends, and—unfortunately—for alleged doping activities, too. As of yet, none of the charges have been proved, but in June of 2012 the United States Anti-Doping Agency (USADA) filed formal charges against Armstrong. The number of accusations that he has been subjected to have billowed into a dark cloud hanging over his career. But however the case turns out, Lance has devoted a lot of time, money, and energy to LAF, which supports cancer research and prevention. That's a great achievement on its own.

Armstrong's fame drew more and more people to the sport. As more people took to riding, word quickly spread that it is a fun and safe way to stay in shape. Doctors often tell athletes recuperating from orthopedic injuries or surgeries to ride their bikes as rehabilitation. In short, Armstrong's career introduced many Americans to the wide world of cycling. His successes meant lots of television coverage, and that's translated into lots of new people enjoying the sport.

CYCLING TODAY

Cycling businesses sell almost twice the number of bikes today that they did in 1981, although the population of the US as a whole has only grown by about a third. The quality and durability of bikes has improved tremendously over the past decade, too. Materials like carbon fiber have made them lighter and stronger than ever. In fact, for $1,200 a well-heeled bike enthusiast can buy a road bike that's actually better than what guys were riding in the Tour de France only fifteen years ago.

Cities, counties, and the federal government are supporting more cycling projects, too, helping to make bike commuting a more popular mode of transportation. As gas prices rise and more people recognize the impacts of climate change, hopefully we'll see people riding bikes for shorter trips and saving their cars only for essential outings.

Technology has also made the sport more fun. Several smartphone apps can track your cycling as you pedal. With them, you can compare your rides against buddies in town, or even keep track of friends riding in other states.

More sophisticated computers and "power meters"—gizmos that measure how many watts you generate when pedaling—now let you keep track of all your training and mileage. And some cycle computers can calculate how much CO_2 (carbon dioxide, the stuff causing global climate change) a rider spares the atmosphere by riding his or her bike instead of driving.

SO...

Biking's come a long way since the boneshaker first hit the scene at the turn of the century! In fact, at this point, the biking "scene" has split up into a diverse array of earth-conscious commuters, fitness advocates, hard-core racers, and just casual groups of tourists and vacationers. So whether you want to conquer the world, save the earth, or just get in shape again, there's a bike—and a biking community—already waiting for you.

2

WHAT'S YOUR BIKE TYPE?

S ince the mid-1860s, people have been touring, racing, and performing tricks on their bikes, and now that you're ready to join the party, it's time to figure out exactly where you fit in.

As you consider several possible biking futures, keep in mind that you don't have to commit to just one type of cycling—you can be lots of different types of cyclists rolled into one. As I write this, I have a mountain bike, a road bike, touring bike, and an efficient and fast town bike out in the garage. Most of my cycling friends have a similar range of bikes at their disposal, and a few have cyclo-cross and jumping bikes, too. There are lots of ways to enjoy cycling, so read on to find the right bike for you.

THE TOWN BIKE—CLEANING UP THE STREETS

A "townie" is just a bike built up to get you from point A to point B. Town bikes come in all shapes and sizes. Many people just adapt an old clunker bike by adding fenders (if they live where there's a lot of snow or rainfall), front and rear lights (mandatory for night riding), and maybe a bell for alerting pedestrians and other cyclists to their oh-so-eco presence.

The emergence of the town bike, or "townie," has helped millions of people get out of their cars and onto their quiet, two-wheeled bikes. Right on! I'm proud to say that in 2011 I pedaled over 850 miles on my townie and spared the atmosphere nearly two hundred pounds of carbon. So just imagine what more bikes on the road could do to improve the environment!

In Bozeman, Montana, and other freezing locales, people often add little spikes to their tires for additional grip on the ice. In Seattle, cyclists have full-coverage fenders on their townies because it rains so much. In Southern California surfers get away with balloon-tire bikes with a single gear—no problem in an area with so few hills; the big tires are also perfect for the sandy beach terrain.

Bikes That Disappear After Your Commute

Folding bikes are just that—bikes with two hinges within the frame. They fold up and can be stashed out of the way on a bus or train, or slotted into a bag for a plane flight. They're popular in Europe, and some commuters in the United States also use them. There are some pretty hip versions out there that ride surprisingly well.

You should look for comfort, safety, and efficiency when choosing the right townie. I have disc brakes on mine for extra braking power because I sometimes haul my kids in a trailer made just for them. I have eight gears for the hills in Colorado; fenders let me ride all winter without getting wet; and my lights keep me safe and visible when it gets dark.

If you're interested in town bikes, look around on the internet to see how people are modifying bikes and what they're using them for. There are limitless options, so all you need to do is get a bike and get going.

You might like a townie if:

- You're worried about rising levels of carbon in the atmosphere
- You'd like to do something about smog and traffic congestion
- You're short on cash and long on dream destinations
- You're willing to spare 10 minutes to enjoy a more relaxing commute

MOUNTAIN BIKES: THE DIRTIER, THE BETTER

Made for riding on trails and featuring wheels that are either 26 or 29 inches in diameter, mountain bikes roll over obstacles and stand up to harsh, off-road riding. They have between eighteen and twenty-four gears, weigh twenty to thirty pounds, have front and rear shocks like a motor-cycle—and are incredibly fun to ride.

The first mass-produced mountain bikes appeared around 1980. By 1990, they were lighter, faster, better performing and, of course, more expensive. Mountain-biking technology has improved steadily ever since, and today they act like giant BMX bikes with gears: They're a blast to ride, very maneuverable, and super comfy—often with both front and rear suspension. They're also among the most durable of bikes. If you're planning on sticking to just one bike, the mountain bike is a solid choice.

Mountain bikes aren't just for the mountains either. Cities like Austin, San Francisco, and Minneapolis all have off-road riding in—or at least nearby to—major urban areas. There are also bike "parks" springing up in places like Seattle.

Some mountain bikes are set up specifically for "downhilling"—a style of mountain biking especially popular at ski areas like Whistler, in Canada. You can ride the lifts up and then ride a downhill course featuring banked corners and jumps. You'll go faster than you ever thought possible on a bike! Downhill bikes have more travel (bigger shocks) for bigger bumps, and beefier frames and wheels. They're durable, but also heavier, making them less than ideal for pedaling uphill.

Mountain bikes are great if you're new to cycling because you can ride them just for fun, use them as commuter bikes, and/or try your hand at racing. Check out USA Cycling (www.usacycling.org/mtb) and the National Interscholastic Cycling Association (nationalmtb.org) if the race scene interests you. It's a lot of fun—and you'll meet tons of people to ride with.

The mountain bike might be for you if:

- You love getting off of the pavement and out into nature
- You enjoy speeding down steep, rocky hills
- You're up for an occasional hop over a rock or bump over a log
- You're looking for one bike to "do it all"

ROAD BIKES: FARTHER AND FASTER

With skinny tires, ultra-light frames, twenty (or more!) gears to choose from, and wheels that are a bit bigger than the wheels on mountain bikes, road bikes cover the miles quickly and at higher speeds than other types of bikes. A Tour de France bike weighs as little as fifteen pounds, but regular road bikes are usually closer to eighteen to twenty-two pounds. Road bikes are fast and never short on fun.

You tend to be slightly bent at the waist when riding a road bike, which puts you in an aerodynamic position. This is important when riding above fifteen miles per hour—and on a road bike, you will be. The road bike's efficiency and speed make descending a curvy road exciting and, with a little training, covering a hundred miles in an afternoon possible.

You sacrifice a little durability and stability with a road bike, however. Its lightweight parts tend to wear out more quickly than the parts on a mountain bike. It's more likely that something will break if you crash or if your bike falls over and hits the pavement, too. Road bikes require a bit more maintenance, so you'll either have to team up with a good bike shop or learn how to do maintenance on the bike yourself, which we'll get to in subsequent chapters. With their skinny tires, road bikes are also more likely to slide on gravel, and the tires will go flat more often than mountain-bike tires. It's nothing you can't manage, but just keep it in mind.

Just like mountain biking, there's a huge race scene for road bikes. Visit USA Cycling (usacycling.org), inquire at your local bike shop, or get on the web and look around. You'll probably find a race nearby, with events for riders of all ages.

Consider a road bike if:

- Riding long distances (say, a hundred miles or more!) sounds like fun
- You like smooth, fast riding
- You follow the Tour de France religiously
- You're serious about fitness

TOURING BIKES—SEE THE WORLD...BY BIKE

On a touring bike, you can ride around the world, bringing along everything you might need. At first glance, touring bikes might look like regular road bikes, but take a closer look, and you'll discover the differences.

Touring bikes help you ride longer distances with extra gear, while keeping you comfortable and able to maintain good speeds. They have the relatively skinny tires (an inch or less wide), large-diameter (twenty-nine inches) wheels, and a long wheelbase (the distance between the wheels); they also have a slightly lower bottom bracket (the part where the cranks go into the frame), and let you sit more upright. These features make touring bikes more stable, more comfortable, and safer, all of which become extremely important when riding with the additional weight of camping gear, spare clothing, and tools.

On long-distance tours there are two ways to carry your stuff. On touring bikes, people have traditionally used "panniers," or saddlebags, to organize and carry equipment for repairs or for camping. These bags mount to racks that bolt directly to the bike's frame. Look for little threaded eyelets on the rear triangle of the bike and the front fork to make sure a bike will accept panniers.

Clean, Quiet, and Cool—"Belt Drive" Bikes

You probably expect that when you see a bicycle, you'll see a chain—but not so fast! "Belt drive" bikes use a belt instead of a chain to power the rear wheel, and they're all the rage lately. The belts are made from polyurethane and carbon and look just like the belt on a car's water pump, but if you look more closely you'll see teeth that mesh with a specialized cog for a bicycle. No oil, no lube—just a quiet and durable system! At this point, they're only widely available on single-speed bikes, but stay tuned.

In the past few years, however, trailers have become an alternative to panniers. These attach to the rear of your bike and roll along behind you. The main advantage of trailers is that they keep the weight off your bike and closer to the ground, which means less mass to affect your steering and balance. Another nice feature is being able to detach your trailer and leave all your equipment at a campsite or hostel (find a safe place and lock it up!). This way you're able to pedal on a lighter bike if you do a side trip.

No matter how you haul your stuff, bike touring is a great way to see the world and meet new people.

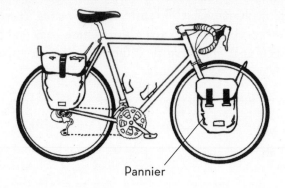

Pannier

You might love a touring bike if:

- Explorers like Marco Polo and Ibn Battuta capture your imagination
- You're not into the whole competition thing
- Camping is your cup of tea
- You'd rather take your time than push the pace

CYCLO-CROSS BIKES: RUN, RIDE, REPEAT

Cyclo-cross is a fun fringe sport that involves running and cycling. Riders compete on a short track with occasional obstacles that require dismounting, running with your bike, and then remounting. Europeans created cyclocross—or "cross" for short—to stay in shape during the winter.

'Cross bikes look like road bikes to the untrained eye, but they actu-ally have slightly fatter tires and more clearance between the tire

Trailer

and the frame for riding in the mud (mud builds up between the wheel and frame, and a 'cross bike lets you keep going, while a road bike

Cyclo-Cross

tends to bog down), and they put the rider in a slightly different position. They're a little heavier than a road bike and offer a bit more stability for riding on grass, dirt, and even snow.

Racing 'cross demands smooth and fast transitions from riding to running and back to riding again. It's pretty easy to learn a decent dismount/re-mount, but doing it at top speed requires a lot of practice. (And I mean a lot.) Serious competitors often reverse their brake levers—meaning that the left lever on the handlebars controls the rear brake—which allows the rider to apply the rear brake when dismounting (since, if you're right-handed, you need to be able to use your right hand to pick up the bike and put it over your shoulder for the run. So keep that in mind if you borrow a bike for a test-ride!

The crazy world of 'cross might be your thing if:

- you love a good workout
- you'll take one intense hour over six leisurely ones
- riding in the cold and wet is no sweat
- you thrive on a challenge

THE TIME TRIAL BIKE—YOUR OWN RACECAR (WITH TWO WHEELS)

Time trial (TT) bikes are specifically built for aerodynamics. In other words, they're made for going fast. A time trial is a bike race in which riders each take a turn on a course. Race officials keep track of every rider's time, and after everyone has completed the course, the fastest time wins.

Because time trial riders are racing alone, the bikes are built for speed over handling, aerodynamics over comfort. These bikes are extremely specialized. Their frames have a more "forward" position, which gives a rider great aerodynamics, but also makes them less comfortable for long hours in the saddle. Features like this make TT bikes less appropriate for commuting or touring. Think of them like a racecar: pretty great to have for those choice occasions when you just want speed, but not the best everyday vehicle.

The time trial bike might be your calling if:

- You love going all-out
- You thrive on competition
- Obsessing over every last detail in the pursuit of speed sounds cool
- The idea of racing alone sounds just fine

TRIATHLON BIKES—SWIM, RIDE, AND RUN

While some people use time-trial bikes in triathlons, a handful of manufacturers make triathlon-specific bikes (or "tri-bikes"). They put the rider in a slightly different position than TT bikes and competition regulations allow them to be lighter. Most folks, though, get by using road bikes with "clip-on" handlebars that create a more aerodynamic position.

In a triathlon, competitors swim first, then ride their bikes for the next leg, and then run for the final part of the race. The idea is the same as any race: Complete the course faster than anyone else. You'll be riding with other competitors on the course, but typically you're not "drafting"—riding closely behind other riders to cut down on wind resistance—in a group, like you see in a bike race, like the Tour de France.

If triathlons become your thing, then someday you may want to pick up a tri-bike or time-trial bike. They are certainly faster than a regular road bike, but until you have the cash for a few different bikes, they're probably too specialized to be your only ride.

You might be the swim-ride-run type if:

- You're always interested in trying something new
- Longer, tougher challenges appeal to you
- Fitness and overall health are important to you
- You're willing to add another sport (or two) to your life

TRACK BIKES—THE VELODROME AND FIXIES

Track riding, another specialized discipline within cycling, offers the speed and tactics of road racing, but on a short (usually 250–400 meters) track with banked corners called a velodrome. You may have seen track events like the match sprint, pursuit, and points race in the Olympics. They're fast and exciting, and there are a variety of races in which to compete.

Track bikes have just one gear. They're also "fixed," meaning you can't coast or freewheel on them. When you're moving, the pedals are always turning. You also use the pedals to brake (track bikes don't have brakes), decreasing your pedal cadence, or RPMs, if you want to slow down.

You'll be klutzy at first, but as soon as you have it down, track cycling can be addictive.

The bikes are light and simple—no brakes, no gears, no derailleurs—just pedals, two wheels, a saddle, handlebars, and a lightweight frame. These bikes, called "fixies" off the velodrome, have become popular with bicycle messengers and other city cyclists.

Over the last decade, the messenger/fixie scene has inspired first urbanites, and now just about everybody, to build up beautiful, stripped-down bikes for tearing around town. Keep in mind, though, that riding a fixie takes some getting used to—especially because of the lack of gears or brakes. Hills and quick stops can be a challenge, especially for a new rider. Some people mount a front brake to their fixie, as a backup to their pedaling.

Fixies are cool because they're so simple, but that also makes them less versatile. Like a TT bike, they're probably not the best choice if you have only one ride, but as a second or third bike—now you're talking.

Think about joining the fixie fad if:

- You don't mind putting in a little extra effort for a little extra credibility
- You've got a minimalist aesthetic
- You bike in an area that's relatively flat
- Your local tattoo parlor already knows you by name

LIFESTYLE BIKES—HELPING YOU LIVE YOUR LIFE

"Lifestyle" bikes, sometimes called "comfort" or "hybrid" bikes, are versatile and stable combinations of the larger, faster wheels of a road bike and the upright and comfortable position of a mountain or town bike.

They come in a variety of shapes and sizes. Some can be ridden on dirt tracks; others are geared toward long bike-path rides.

Lifestyle bikes offer the fitness benefits of cycling along with plenty of comfort—and they're durable enough to serve as commuter bikes and work for occasional trips around town as well. If you think you might enjoy cycling, but aren't going to make it your primary activity, a lifestyle bike might be the right ride for you.

Look for a lifestyle bike if:

- You couldn't care less about racing
- The idea of jumping logs and hopping rocks sounds ridiculous
- An hour on the bike path is just about right

CARGO BIKES: TRANSPORTING YOUR LIFE

The Dutch and Danish practically live on their bikes. The Netherlands and Denmark are cold in the winter but have very few hills, which means lots of easy cycling. Consequently, families and businesses sometimes have "cargo" bikes, or bikes with various storage boxes and racks for transporting everything from books to babies to building materials.

Heavy, practical, and expensive, a cargo bike can be a great addition to your garage if you need a clean, inexpensive form of transportation for your lifestyle or business. They come in every configuration you can imagine, too: Some have a huge box in the front for carrying everything from ice cream to work supplies to your pet dog. Others have an extended rear end, letting you put groceries in bags or racks on the side, have a buddy hop on (be careful!) for a quick ride, or haul your gear to soccer practice. As long as you're not transporting large farm animals or gold bars, a cargo bike can make your life roll a little more smoothly.

A cargo bike might be for you if:

- ⬤ You love the next new thing
- ⬤ Taking care of the environment is a priority of yours
- ⬤ You always have a project going that requires you to haul things around
- ⬤ You'll take a pick-up truck over a sports car any day

BMX AND PARK/STREET BIKES: RISKY BUSINESS

The popular story is that BMX—a shortened term for "bicycle moto-cross"—began in Southern California in the late 1960s. People say that kids there wanted to imitate the loud, powerful off-road motorcycles of the day and began riding their bikes on homemade tracks with jumps and banked turns. The sport caught on, and by the late '70s manufacturers were building bikes with tough frames for jumping and knobby tires for gripping the dirt.

Most of this is true—but it wasn't the '60s and it wasn't SoCal. As early as 1956, in Holland, of all places, kids were racing their bikes in the dirt. These Dutch youth, just like their California counterparts, thought racing

BMX

motorcycles was cool, so they imitated the sport on their small-wheeled, motorless bikes. And BMX was born.

It's not clear if any of the California pioneers knew of the Dutch BMXers, but whatever the case, BMX became a worldwide phenomenon thanks to the SoCal riders of the '60s. By the early '70s, they started copying their skateboarding buddies riding empty swimming pools. The pools featured smooth riding surfaces, flowing transitions from shallow to deep ends, and curved landings—perfect for making jumps. Magazines like *Bicycle Motocross News* sprang up.

Competitive BMX took the United States by storm, and by 1977 it gave rise to the world's leading race scene. BMX continued as a fringe sport in Europe, and it never became the rage as it did in the states. Today, there's a BMX world championship, and BMX is also an Olympic sport, with participants hailing from Australia, Japan, most of the tries, and beyond.

BMX bikes usually have twenty-inch wheels, so they're smaller and more maneuverable than mountain bikes. Jumping, park, and street bikes (like that ridden by YouTube sensation Danny MacAskill see page 40) are similar in design but usually have larger wheels. Riders prefer these larger wheels because they're more stable and they maintain their speed a little better. More and more kids are getting into street and park bikes, but the larger wheels are more suited for riders who are five feet or taller.

If mountain biking and BMX had babies, they'd be park and street riding. These gnarly disciplines harness the larger wheels and frames of mountain biking, but the simplicity and maneuverability of BMX. The bikes allow riders to jump bigger, roll faster, and conquer obstacles that would thwart a BMX or mountain bike.

While each has its specific attributes, BMX, park, and street bikes have some elements in common: They have a single gear, and are lightweight, fast, and ideal for jumping and trick riding. They're also unbelievably tough and pretty cheap compared to mountain bikes.

On the flip side, these bikes don't have gears for going uphill, and with smaller wheels they don't easily cover long distances like a road or mountain bike does. They're great for bombing around dirt fields and

Get to Know: Danny MacAskill

Though he may not be a household name (yet), Scottish sensation Danny MacAskill has become a YouTube phenomenon. As of December 2012, his most popular post has thirty-one million views. He's a "trials" or "street" rider, meaning he has a bike specifically made for tricks and jumping. The guy launches over stairs, rides along walls, hops fences, and basically goes huge on the bike.

MacAskill was born on the Isle of Skye, in Scotland. When his video hit big, he was working as a bike mechanic. Since then, he's quit his job to ride full time and has sponsorships with Red Bull and Inspired Bicycles. He's also been nominated for awards like the *National Geographic* Adventurer of the Year.

tracks with your friends, but for getting across town they're less efficient. If you're considering a BMX bike as your first or only bike, then make sure you take these pros and cons into account.

BMX bikes are a great way to get into cycling, and if you're competitive, there's a thriving race scene across the country. Check out the National

Bicycle League (www.nbl.org) and the American Bicycling Association (www.ababmx.com) for more info. Chances are there's a BMX track near you—and a bunch of kids riding out there right now.

You might be a BMXer if:

- You're always trying to go harder, faster, and stronger
- Battle scars are just part of your schtick
- You listen to thrash metal
- You'll take skateboarding over roller skating seven days a week

TRIAL BIKES: LOOK OUT FOR THOSE STAIRS!

Trials is probably the least practical and most extreme style of cycling. It's equal parts BMX, freestyle, and lunacy. Trials riders maneuver their bikes up and down obstacles like picnic tables, staircases, and boulders. They also perform tricks like huge bunny-hops (lifting or hopping their bikes over stuff like trash cans and fences), riding wheelies on their front or rear wheel, and throwing 360s (complete rotations) and flips. Scottish rider Danny MacAskill is part trials master, part nuts, and part king-slayer in the "terrain park," a dirt and concrete version of a snowboard or ski park.

The typical trials bike has twenty-inch wheels, a super-stout frame, and wide, squishy tires for grip. Trials bikes also have a single, tiny gear, which means you won't be pedaling anywhere fast on these. What you can do, though, is hop, jump, and pedal over obstacles that seem impossible to overcome at first. A dedicated trials bike also ditches its saddle so you can hop the bike and sit way back over the rear wheel when going down a steep hill without the saddle getting in the way. Again, trials bikes are impractical for everyday riding, but unique features make it possible for them do what other bikes can't.

Trail Bike

Most riders who are interested in trying out trials start out by modifying a twenty-six-inch-wheel mountain bike rather than going straight to a true trials bike. They strip off the gears and derailleurs, do away with the suspension, lower the saddle, and start perfecting their techniques. Later on, if they're still into it, some of them build up a dedicated trials bike, though others would rather have the larger wheels and bigger gear of the adapted mountain bike. Check out Trials-Online.com for more info.

Jump on to a trials bike if:

- A little tumble doesn't bother you
- Trying the "impossible" sounds like fun
- The harder it is, the more you dig it
- You're more of a martial artist than a visual artist

LOW RIDERS—THEY DRIVE A LITTLE SLOWER

Some of the most ornate and tricked out bikes ever built, low riders are part bike and part artwork. They use twenty-inch wheels like a BMX bike, usually have a long, narrow "banana" seat, and feature tons of chrome. You can't tour on them, you'll never jump one, they don't descend well, and, to be honest, they're no good at going uphill. *But* if you dig the look, then they can be some of the coolest bikes out there. Flashy, relaxed, and slow-moving, low riders aren't for everybody, but if you're only riding short distances and you enjoy upgrading and tinkering with bikes, maybe you should think about one.

The original low riders first arrived on the scene as a way for kids to imitate low-riding cars. The idea of course has come a long way since then, and now some people have taken the idea so far that the bikes are barely rideable. With tons of chrome and funky accessories, they're more statements on style than they are useful bicycles. Search a bit on the internet and see what you can find. Maybe there are some low riders in your area. (And trust me, if there are, they won't be hard to spot.)

Get on down with a low rider if:

- You'll take chrome over colors
- Tricked-out vehicles catch your eye
- You're a collector at heart
- You love upgrading and pimping out your ride

TANDEMS AND RECUMBENTS, AND TRIKES— KEEPING YOU OFF THE BEATEN PATH

If none of the bikes above turn your crank, then consider something a little more unusual. How about a tandem—a bike built for two riders? They're fun and a great way to pedal with a buddy. You could also try a recumbent, where you sit as if you're in a chair and the pedals are in front of you. These can be easier to balance than a two-wheeler and more comfortable if you're riding for several hours. There are even three- and four-wheeled bikes, if you have a physical issue that prevents you from riding a traditional, two-wheeled machine.

Tandems are probably the most common of these outlying bicycle types. On flat terrain, two riders can absolutely fly along, covering more ground than a "normal" single-rider bike. The rider in front, called the "captain," must be in sync with his "stoker," or the rider on the rear saddle. It takes some practice and coordination to get smooth with your partner, but it's pretty cool watching a duo riding along at twenty-five miles-per-hour for hours on end.

Consider trying one of these bikes if:

- You take "weird" as a compliment
- You like to stand out in a crowd
- You're willing to adapt, just to get into cycling
- You've tried "old-school" bicycling and it's just not for you— but you're still into the idea of propelling yourself forward on a human-powered vehicle

Still haven't found what you're looking for? Get creative on the web or start asking around—if you don't see a bike meant for you, learn how to build one!

My Favorite Bikes

By Lennard Zinn

In the thirty-two years I have been building bikes, and in the fifty years I've been riding them, I've ridden and built a lot of bikes. Some of them particularly stand out.

My Schwinn Stingray with a banana seat, ape-hanger handlebars, and a sissy bar gave me freedom, as it got me all over the neighborhoods and canyon trails near my home in Los Alamos, New Mexico.

My sixty-four-centimeter fully Campagnolo-equipped, steel, lugged Masi road bike was the perfect tool for my budding racing career. I won the 1980 Durango-to-Silverton Iron Horse Classic road race on that bike, setting the course record. It went downhill fast without high-speed shimmy (common in tall bikes). It was sad when I bent it up in a crash.

The first mountain bike I rode was Tom Ritchey's personal bike in 1981 while I was working for him building Ritchey bikes. It was steel with smooth, fillet-brazed joints and no suspension. I took a long, painful (when landing) flyer over the handlebars down the first steep hill I came to as I discovered—too late—that Tom's brakes were hooked up "moto-style": The right hand controlled the front brake, and vice versa—the opposite of how bikes are normally set up, which is what I was used to and expected.

The first bike I made for myself was a sixty-five centimeter lugged steel road bike that finally fit my long body correctly. I painted it with flames, and it was the fastest, most stable bike I'd ever had.

My first full-suspension mountain bike was the original Zinn "Megabike," a three-inch-travel model with twenty-six-inch wheels. It was painted like a tiger shark, and it allowed me to ride much faster on rough downhills than any bike before. When I then made the first 29er Megabike (a mountain bike with twenty-nine-inch wheels), I could clean (ride without putting my foot down) steep, rocky climbs that I never had before, and I could go yet faster on rough trails, whether uphill, downhill, or level. Now I have a 29er Megabike with a fourteen-speed Rohloff internal-gear hub and a Gates belt-drive instead of a chain—in snow and freezing cold or in deep mud, the drivetrain stays clean, and it shifts perfectly, while my riding buddies' bikes are so clogged with ice or mud and grass that they can't shift.

Every fall, my favorite bikes are my two identical (for bike changes during muddy races) Zinn magnesium cyclo-cross bikes. They are super light and very smooth when riding rough courses, especially when they are outfitted with tubular knobby tires inflated to low pressure (twenty-nine pounds per square inch, or psi).

I love traveling all over the world with my Zinn titanium bike that has four screw-together couplers on the frame and one on the handlebar stem. Within a matter of minutes, I can take it apart and pack it into a small case that flies with me for free, and when I get to my destination, I have a no-compromise, lightweight racing bike that fits me perfectly. If you've ever tried renting or borrowing a decent bike that fits well when you're 6'5" tall, then you can understand why I love this bike so much.

When I ride in the mountains around Boulder in the summer, my magnesium road bike is my favorite steed. It's the lightest bike I've ever had, it's custom-made to fit me perfectly, it handles like a dream, and it soaks up vibration so I can ride in comfort all day long.

I love riding the redrock trails in Moab and Sedona on my white, red, and black Zinn Gigabike six-inch-travel 29er. It's beautiful (it's on the cover of the fifth edition of Zinn and the Art of Mountain Bike Maintenance), and it smoothes out the bumps so I can ride fast down rocky trails that I'd be crawling down on any other bike.

Lastly, there's nothing like tooling along Hawaiian beaches in style on a heavy cruiser bike with balloon tires! Its curves look good, and it feels great to just cruise with no hurry.

Lennard Zinn is one of the most respected framebuilders and cycling journalists in the world today. He's built just about every kind of bike imaginable. He's the author of Zinn and the Art of Road Bike Maintenance *and its companion volume* Zinn and the Art of Mountain Bike Maintenance. *Highly recommended for the do-it-yourself mechanic!*

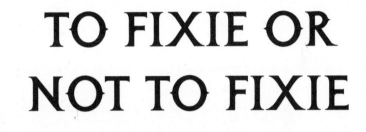

3

TO FIXIE OR NOT TO FIXIE

S tripped down, super fast, and totally gorgeous—fixies do away with gears, multiple rear cogs, and derailleurs in favor of simplicity and speed. And although we talked about them a bit in the last chapter, fixies have caught on to such a degree that it's worth talking about them in even more detail—how they work, why they're popular, and what it is that all these fixie fanatics seem to have in common.

THE EARLY YEARS

Track cyclists have been racing and riding fixies for over a century, but it's really bike messengers who popularized them. In the early 1980s, many messengers adopted the fixie because of its light weight, durability, and ease of maintenance. Without gears, derailleurs, or brakes, there's less to break or get out of whack. It's the perfect urban assault vehicle.

Bike messengers haven't always been the tattooed, pierced road warriors we know today. Messengers have been around almost as long as the modern bike, but in the 1980s they basically became their own underground tribe, dressing in tall argyle socks, military fatigues, and baggy cut-off jeans cinched with studded leather belts, reminiscent of the '70s and '80s punk scene. Despite riding in traffic all day, many went without helmets.

Their fixies were all over the map, too—in terms of appearance. Some were wrapped in black electrical tape, which served a dual purpose: to protect the bike from scratches and conceal the bike's brand, and therefore value, from thieves. On the flip side, some messengers proudly—though they might not have admitted it—displayed old-school track frames, kitted out with street-adapted gear like outdated "cow-horn" handlebars. Either way, mainstream riders took notice, and they began to emulate the messengers.

THE FIXIE SCENE

Fast forward to today. You can't swing a dead cat without hitting a fixie—or a skinny hipster riding one. In the bike world, fixies and the associated style are the trendiest things going.

The fixie culture influence shows up in everything from the informal messenger races, called "Alley Cats," and epic parties hosted by groups like "Dead Baby" in Seattle, "Rat Patrol" in Chicago, and "Skidmarxxx" in Austin, to the messenger-style bags sold at Gap and Saks Fifth Avenue. Fixie culture encompasses everything from underground racing to messenger work to bike collecting. It's a fun, irreverent universe. It's mostly urban in nature, but that doesn't mean you can't dig it if you live on a farm or in Tinytown, USA.

If you're interested in learning more about fixie culture, first go online. Bike blogs, information about messenger races (including a world championship), Tumblr feeds, and insider folklore will keep you occupied for weeks.

BEFORE ALL ELSE: THE BAG

A samurai has a sword, a cowboy has a gun, and a messenger has a bag. You've seen 'em—the utilitarian bags slung over the shoulders of hipster speedsters everywhere. What started as an urban "look" has become cool no matter where you live or what you do. In fact, by the look of things, most messenger bags sold today go to people who barely ride—that's how popular the messenger look is. Though simple, the bags are perfectly adapted to delivering mail and packages by bike. With a single shoulder strap and

LE MESSENGER

a rectangular, usually waterproof, main compartment, these bags ride in the center of a cyclist's back. A small waist-strap keeps them from sliding off the back when pedaling. When a messenger makes a stop, she or he unclasps the waist belt and then slides the bag around to the front, without lifting it off the shoulder. Then the messenger peels back a fold-over flap and removes whatever letter or package he or she is delivering. Quick and easy to use, and super durable, the messenger bag is so popular because it works so well and because it becomes a personalized part of its wearer. Choose a bag you like and start using it. In no time, you'll have a trusted companion for school, work, errands, and racing around town.

THE ANTI-UNIFORM

Messengers typically ride in some of the least practical and funkiest clothing you'll ever see on a bike. In a way, it's the anti-uniform—everybody looks different and there are no rules.

One way messengers break the mold is with their helmets. Look out for hockey helmets, "hair nets" (or old-school, padded leather, protective headwear from the '70s and beyond), skate helmets, or nothing at all. Once I even saw a woman riding with a wreath of flowers on her head (low protection factor, but kinda cute). Experiment with style all you like, but riding with an unprotected cranium is not something you want to emulate. Another thing that safe riders generally have in common is some way of keeping fabric away from their gears. That means shorts, skirts, or a rubber band or some other kind of stay to keep baggy pants from getting caught (and ruined) by the chain and chainrings.

As for clothing, head to your local vintage shop and see what grabs your eye. Don't worry if you've never seen another soul riding in your chosen purple-pleather chaps—if you can ride in 'em, then more pedal power to you.

By the same token, don't feel like you've got to impress anybody or try to make a statement. Sometimes not making a statement is a statement.

PROTECT YOUR INVESTMENT

The bike lock is another messenger accessory. Some messengers opt for the tiny "u-lock" stashed in a rear pocket, while others have a clunky chain worn around the waist like a belt, joined by a lock. There are several options, to be sure, but just make sure your lock is as tough as possible if you're pedaling in a busy city or a college town. Thieves love a good bike, and come to think of it, sometimes any bike—so watch out.

TRICKS OF THE TRADE

Lockless—What to Do

Sooner or later you'll find yourself out on a ride and without a lock. Bummer, but all is not lost. What you need to do in this situation is make it harder for a would-be thief to jump on your bike and dash away. Here are two quick tricks to make it a bit more difficult for him or her. First, remove your front wheel from the frame if you can. Lay the front wheel against the frame, then take your helmet and clip the chin strap through the front wheel and around the frame. If you can't remove your front wheel, then just use your helmet's chin strap to clip the front wheel to the frame, so it won't roll. In either configuration, a thief would have to unclip your helmet (and reinstall the front wheel if you removed it) before making a getaway. It's not a sure-fire fix, but it'll slow somebody down so you have time to holler for help, call the cops, or just shame the dastardly thief into leaving your ride alone!

CHOOSING YOUR FIXIE

Before you start hunting for a fixie, here are a few ideas to consider. First off: brakes. Many fixies, as well as true track bikes, do not have hand brakes—you control your speed with your pedaling. Spin your legs faster and you go faster. If you need to slow down, you decrease your pedaling cadence. If you're an experienced rider, you can unweight your back end and stop pedaling as you do so. This stops the rear wheel. Then, if you keep your legs locked when you re-weight the wheel, you skid along, effectively braking your rear wheel. It may sound a little complicated, if not risky, but with some practice you can do it. Hop on to YouTube and search for "how to ride a fixie," and you'll find bunches of posts, some of them even helpful!

Having, at minimum, a front brake on the bike is a good idea, especially when you're first learning to ride a fixie. (You can certainly have a rear brake, too.) You'll be safer, and it helps control your speed. It works just like a regular front brake, except that in this case you use it to augment your pedaling action in order to slow down. Many riders, once they're comfortable, remove this front brake and rely only on their pedaling for braking.

Keep in mind that some states have laws about riding bikes without hand brakes. I've never heard of anybody being ticketed for riding a fixie, but heads up—it's possible that Johnny Law could pull you over.

CONVERTING YOUR BIKE

It is possible to convert a "geared" bike—a bike with gears, derailleurs, and shifters—into a fixie, but it does take some mechanical expertise and know-how.

If you're interested, you'll need a frame with "horizontal dropouts." The dropout is the slot into which your rear wheel fits. Almost all road, 'cross, and touring frames have "vertical" dropouts these days. Fixies and BMX bikes, on the other hand, still come with horizontal dropouts. A horizontal dropout runs parallel to the ground, and you slide the wheel in from the back of the frame unlike a vertical dropout, into which you pull the wheel up and back.

If you don't have horizontal dropouts it becomes very complicated to convert a frame to a fixie. I'd recommend either finding a frame with horizontal dropouts, or purchasing an entire bike, ready to go. Converting a frame with vertical dropouts into a fixie is probably more hassle than you're willing to endure.

PEDALING TECHNIQUE

You've found a fixie and maybe even inherited a battered messenger bag. Before you shave a mohawk on your head or schedule an appointment with your tattoo artist, let's get up to speed on some fixie technique.

Surviving the Corners

The most obvious difference between a fixie and other bikes is that you'll be pedaling the entire time you're moving—that includes corners, which you'd usually be coasting through. If you're really flying on the bike, you tend to lean in a corner, too, which means your inside pedal comes closer to the road surface. Lean far enough and your pedal can hit the pavement, which causes the bike to jump. On a fixie, this usually means crashing.

For your first few fixie rides, take your bike to an empty parking lot or even a grass field with firm ground. Pedal around for about a half-hour become accustomed to the habit of always moving your legs. Weird, eh?

My first time on a track bike, I did a few laps on the velodrome and really thought I had it perfected—until I forgot to pedal and the back end of that bike hopped like a mule stung by a hornet. Lifetime uncool moment number 8,549 for me.

Once you're comfortable, start taking corners with a little more speed. Wear your helmet and maybe even some gloves in case you fall off. Pedaling the corners may feel risky at first, but with some practice you'll get it. Just stay within your comfort range, and don't try to go too fast at first.

Surviving Traffic

Riding a fixie means planning ahead. Some riders liken it to chess—the good players think six and eight moves ahead, rather than just reacting to their opponent's last move. A fixie can't stop on a dime like other bikes can, so you need to be scanning the road ahead for approaching cars, obstacles, funky turns, and changing stoplights. You'll need to divide your attention between what's happening right where you are and the upcoming landscape. It's quite a challenge. Avoid busy intersections and roads, particularly when you're just starting out, and keep playing a few moves ahead.

The Trackstand

Maybe you've seen a cyclist arrive at a stoplight, and, rather than taking a foot off a pedal and putting it down, she chooses to balance on her bike. This is called a "trackstand."

In an event on the track called the match sprint, two riders go head to head to see who's the fastest over a thousand meters. Sometimes both riders will try to take the second position, hoping their rival will sprint first so they can jump behind and save energy by drafting off the leader.

If both riders want to be in the second position, they'll slow to crawl and occasionally stop completely—in a trackstand—trying to get the opponent to roll ahead. It's a tense, fun moment in the race.

When you try it, you'll discover it's actually easier to do a trackstand on a fixie than on a freewheel bike. You can pedal backward and the bike rolls backward, then pedal forward and you'll creep forward. A bike with a freewheel only pedals forward, so when you ride one you're constantly inching ahead, then catching yourself with your brakes. Doing a trackstand on a fixie holds you steady at a stoplight, where on a freewheel bike you're always inching into the intersection. Learning to trackstand is a fun and useful skill (and let's face, it looks cool, too)—after just a few hours of practice, you'll be "riding" in place.

ALLEY CATS

Messenger clubs often hold "Alley Cats," or bike races specifically geared for fixie pilots. The first modern races were held in the '80s, though messengers had raced periodically since the turn of the twentieth century. An Alley Cat mimics a day in the life of a messenger, with stops every so often at different locations on an urban course. In an Alley Cat, competitors show up, get a "manifest," or a list of all the stops they'll need to make, and then have a few minutes to plot the fastest course that hits all of them. Being a local is a definite advantage.

There's even a Cycle Messenger World Championships, sanctioned by the International Federation of Bike Messengers Associations. Cities like Chicago and Berlin have hosted the event. If the annual race is anywhere near you, go check it out—these riders are fast.

Don't expect to find Tour de France riders at an Alley Cat though some riders' race numbers are often just playing cards (originally they were tarot cards) jammed in the riders' spokes. The events are way less orga-nized than the Tour, but they're open to a wider swath of participants and, in my observation, much more fun.

If you have a messenger service in your city or town, ask them about an Alley Cat, or search the Web—but be warned, these races take place on open courses with traffic. I'd recommend going and watching, rather than racing among the cars. As for me, you'll find me on the curb, not out with these brave (crazy?) souls.

WHERE TO GO FOR MORE INFO

Still interested? Lucky for you there's information out there if you look. Try and rent the documentary *Red Light Go*, a fun glimpse of fixie culture. There are also a few books out there, including *Fixed: Global Fixed-Gear Bike Culture* by Andrew Edwards and Max Leonard.

My advice, though, is poke around for other fixie fanatics in your area and give it a go.

The Bike Snob NYC

The Bike Snob: blogger extraordinaire, wordsmith, outlaw, and opinionated cycling geek. For years he concealed his identity from those around him, even his then-girlfriend, now-wife and mother of his only child. Only a few enlightened cognoscenti knew his real name, but it wasn't until the Snob wrote/published a book that he had to voluntarily "out" himself.

Eben Weiss, at the age of thirty-six, revealed himself as the Bike Snob in 2010.

And really nothing has changed. Eben writes the funniest, most perceptive, most spot-on cycling commentary you'll read, anywhere. He lives in Brooklyn, so often he's up to his bottom bracket in fixie culture, much of which he lampoons and a fair bit he celebrates.

You can read his daily posts at bikesnobnyc.blogspot.com, and I promise, you will not be disappointed. He tackles everything from goofy folks he encounters while commuting in the city, to the latest edition of the Tour de France, to developments in equipment.

You can read his stuff in *Bicycling* magazine or pick up either of his books (*The Bike Snob*, and *The Enlightened Cyclist*), but his best work appears on his blog. Bookmark it on your browser and check back daily. You're welcome!

A Word on Tension

by Rob Copollillo

If you're riding a fixie then you need to consider chain tension. Because your fixie will not have gears or a derailleur, there's no need for the bike to have the additional chain to accommodate longer gears. Part of what a derailleur does is take up the slack when you're riding a "shorter," or easier, gear. That's one reason why there's a big spring in your derailleur—so it can tension the chain when there would normally be slack in it.

Your fixie will have a fixed-length chain, so you'll need to adjust chain tension, which can be done in a few different ways. The horizontal dropouts on a fixie (or BMX frame) make chain tensioning easy because you can simply slide your wheel forward or backward to get the right tension.

And what is the "right tension"? This is a little tough to figure out at first. You want your chain as tight as it can be without making it difficult to spin the pedals slowly forward. Any looser than this and your chain can come off (danger!).

You'll want to pull the rear wheel back in the dropouts until it is tight against the chain. Tighten the rear-wheel bolts a bit. Now, slowly turn the crank forward with light pressure. Let go and see if the wheel and cranks keep turning, or if they bind and stop. If the latter occurs, then your chain is a bit too tight. Loosen the bolts and slide the rear wheel forward a millimeter, retighten, and perform the above test again. Once the cranks continue to turn without binding or stopping, you're there. Tighten the bolts and get going.

Don't let anybody sell you on the idea of a "chain tensioner"; this little gizmo works great on a single-speed bike, but it's not right for a fixie. A chain tensioner can't handle the stress of a fixie's drivetrain, so don't even try—it's dangerous and it won't work.

Other Types of Tension

There are a few other methods for tensioning a chain if you don't have horizontal dropouts, but they're a bit complicated. Some bikes have an "eccentric" bottom bracket, which means you can rotate the bottom bracket within the frame to take slack out of the chain. White Industries makes a hub that does the same.

The bottom bracket and the hub are intricate, specialized pieces of equipment (and they're heavy), so I'd recommend you find a frame with horizontal dropouts and go traditional, rather than trying either of these. If you decide to try either eccentric option, you'll need a skilled mechanic's help, so ask at your local shop.

Chainline

Right behind chain tension in the galaxy of fixie importance is "chainline." On a geared bike your chain moves side to side between gears, which means it's usually not in perfect alignment with the front chainrings. This is no big deal—it's the price we pay for having all those gear options. On a fixie, though, you want your chain perfectly lined up between the rear cog and the front chainring. It's stronger this way, more efficient, and has less of a tendency to fall off.

You can adjust chainline several different ways, including adding/removing spacers (on the hub or bottom bracket axles), "redishing" the rear wheel, or adjusting the bottom bracket side to side. These are manageable, but somewhat complicated procedures that demand a lot of trial and error. Ask your local bike shop for assistance.

4

FINDING
YOUR RIDE

Buying a bike is like buying a piece of clothing: It has to fit, it has to say something about who you are, and you have to feel comfortable with it.

You're probably not working with an unlimited budget, so, fortunately, there are a ton of great places to buy an affordable bike, from the corner bike shop to a bike swap to the internet. But before you get going, it's worth spending some time to figure out which avenue is the best for you.

Bikes have gotten really strong, really light, and—in terms of quality— relatively inexpensive over the last couple decades. Sure, you can spend $15,000 on the latest and greatest ultralight, uberstrong ride, but you really don't need to. For one-tenth of that amount (or less) you can purchase a race-ready road or mountain bike with no problem. And you can spend much less if you choose to purchase a used bike.

Do an honest assessment of how much you can spend, and start saving. When you're making your budget, remember that you're not just buying a bike. You're going to need a helmet, lights, a basic tool kit, and maybe a messenger bag or other accessories, too.

When it comes to bikes, you tend to get what you pay for, particularly when you're buying new. Beware, though, of a deal that seems too good or of new technology that seems too "cutting edge" to be true. Don't let anybody pressure you into a "deal of a lifetime," either. Buy what fits your lifestyle and what will work for you, not the coolest brand or what your favorite cyclist rides.

You need a good, reliable bike, so be realistic and aim for an affordable starter model. Down the road you can worry about custom bikes and saving forty grams on a handmade set of carbon-fiber wheels.

Crush Hour

No matter what kind of bike you buy or where you get it, you need to take care of it. That means regular maintenance, but it also means keeping it out of harm's way. Never leave your bike leaning on or lying behind a car. All kinds of great bikes have met their maker way too soon after unwitting drivers have backed up over them. Always leave your bike somewhere visible and, if the area is at all sketchy, locked up, too!

A BIKE'S INGREDIENTS: CARBON, BAMBOO, AND BERYLLIUM

For the first hundred years of the bike's existence, frames were built from one material: steel. Steel works well. It is durable, can be easily repaired, and gives a comfortable ride. Soon, though, brainiac designers began trying to improve on steel, and began experimenting with newer materials like aluminum, carbon fiber, titanium, and even natural products like bamboo.

For your first bike, don't get suckered into feeling like you need astrophysics-grade high-modulus carbon (but if you find a good deal on a frame made of the stuff, buy it—quick!). Every material has its strengths and weaknesses; here's a quick run-down on what bike frames are made of, and what that means for you, the rider.

Steel

Tried and true, and relatively easy to repair if gets bent. Steel also absorbs road vibration. It's comfortable and relatively inexpensive.

Aluminum

Lightweight, strong, and relatively inexpensive, but it also fatigues over time, and can't be easily repaired. It's a bit less comfortable than other materials, as it's very rigid. Makes a great entry-level bike, though.

Titanium

Extremely light, practically unbreakable, and it flexes a bit so it's comfortable, but it's way more expensive than aluminum or steel. Great for travel because it's tough, corrosion-proof, and comfortable.

Carbon Fiber

Most of the serious innovation in bike technology over the past decade has been in carbon fiber. It's ridiculously light, extremely strong, and absorbs shock very well. However, it's expensive to develop, can be damaged when traveling, and it's probably not the best for decades-long durability.

Bamboo

No, really. Bamboo's actually pretty strong, but bamboo bikes are expensive and their long-term durability is still unproven.

Beryllium, AerMet, Composites

These were the rage in the '90s, but they fell out of favor for a variety of reasons. Avoid these and rare or funky materials like Russian titanium. If it's way cheaper than the other stuff, chances are it's no good. Don't get swindled!

In general, don't stress out over your frame material. If you buy a new bike by a reputable brand, or a well maintained used bike, you'll be fine with steel, aluminum, carbon, or titanium. I've ridden all of them, and if I was slower than the competition on any of them, it had zero to do with the bike and everything to do with me! Again, fit, comfort, and reliability should trump frame material for your first bike.

KIDS' AND WOMEN'S BIKES

Maybe you have an idea of the right material for you, but before you hit the pavement (figuratively speaking), keep in mind that some manufacturers build bikes with slightly different shapes and measurements geared toward women and kids. Once upon a time, women, kids, and smaller riders were left to suffer on bikes sized for average, adult men—no longer!

Women tend to have slightly shorter torsos, longer legs (relative to overall body size), and smaller hands than men do. Thankfully, most big brands design their women's models with these facts in mind, so the bikes fit better and ride more comfortably than ever.

Kids' bikes have inherited many of the technological advances of their parents' bikes, making them lighter (really important for smaller riders—imagine if your bike weighed one-third of your body weight!) and with better handling.

An adult women's model might be the perfect solution for teenagers, male or female, who might not be fully "adult-sized," but who may also have outgrown a kids' bike. Even if you're a guy, don't be weird about buying women's components (like brake levers) or a frame if it works for you. If it fits, you'll have way more fun on it! And if you're a woman, then take advantage of modern designs catering to your body and its dimensions.

RIDE BEFORE YOU BUY

Enough with all this talk about materials and frames, let's get down to actually buying a bike! Before you hand over your life savings to a smooth-talking salesperson, spend some time trying to ride as many bikes as you can. Borrowing from friends and test-riding at shops will give you a sense of what you might like, so that when you finally lay down your cash, it won't be for the wrong bike.

FINDING A BIKE SHOP YOU CAN TRUST

Bike shops are really important, but good bike shops are what really matter. There really is quite a bit of difference amongst shops these days. Do your homework on the web and ask friends in order to find the best one in your area. It will save you hassle, time, and money. Chances are you'll meet some cool riders through a good shop, too.

Once you find the right spot, you'll have a place to get advice and maybe even buy your bike. Having a good shop in your corner tilts the odds in your favor. They'll tell you if and when they're having sales, and sometimes shops will even have a message board where cyclists who are selling their bikes can post ads. If you find a used bike, you can take it to the shop and have a good mechanic check it over before you shell out your cash.

A shop should help you through the bike-buying process, even if you find your bike elsewhere. Why? In treating you right, they'll make a long-term customer out of you. Maybe you'll buy a helmet or some other equipment there. When something on your new bike needs an adjustment or a repair, you'll probably be taking your business to your chosen shop. And down the road, you'll eventually buy another bike, and this time it might just be at the shop that helped you out.

End-of-Season Sales

Bike shops operate a bit like car dealerships. Bikes come in before the big riding season (spring through fall), and during the winter leftover inventory usually gets sold at a discount. Ask about end-of-season sales at your shop. Maybe that bike you've been eyeing will cost 20 percent less if you wait a few months.

Five Things Every Bike Shop Should Do

1. Make you feel welcome and comfortable
2. Explain things as thoroughly or as simply as you need them to
3. Listen: The staff should help you get what you want and what you need, and not steer you toward some high-priced alternative or upgrade
4. Help you find the perfect fit on your bike—and keep trying if they haven't got it yet
5. Offer to swap out saddles, stems, and handlebars to get you comfortable

NEW VERSUS USED

You've done your homework, you know what you're looking for, and you're ready to buy. Fantastic! In just a few days, you'll be riding off into the future with your friends. If you have the cash, then you're probably considering something new. That's great because a new bike offers some considerable advantages, like dialing the fit to your body from day one.

Going used is a great way to save some cash, but you'll need to do your homework. Any time you get on a used bike, you're essentially inheriting the original owner's fit. Sometimes that's no problem, but it's rare that someone else's position fits you perfectly. Make sure a used bike can be fit to your body, rather than contorting your body to fit the bike. If you get close to making a purchase, ask the bike's current owner if it's cool to take the bike to a shop to have it checked for soundness, and also to have somebody experienced verify you'll be able to get comfortable on it.

Whether you buy new or used, hopefully you've found the best shop in your area, so that they can help get you set up by changing stems and handlebars, and positioning the saddle.

SHOPPING ONLINE

Shopping on the internet is a blessing and a curse. While browsing, you can shop from thousands of people you wouldn't meet at a bike swap or at a race, so you get a fabulous selection. The flip side, though, is your inability to touch, see, or test ride what you're buying. As long as you keep this in mind, it's still possible to shop online—just do it cautiously.

Craigslist, eBay, Amazon, and the Classifieds

It's a big, crazy world out there online, so start surfing and see what you come up with. Craigslist, eBay, and Amazon are the obvious choices, but you'll also find a good selection of used bikes on cycling sites like TheBikeTraderOnline.com or RecycledCycles.net.

Most sellers are willing to send you measurements, so if you see a bike you might like but have questions about its size, you can ask for seat-tube or top-tube lengths. If you have a friend's or sibling's bike, then you can measure against it to get a sense of the other bike's size. Is it longer, shorter, taller? How will that feel in comparison to the bikes you've already ridden? These are things to think about before you buy.

Though the internet gives you access to great deals and to bikes in faraway places, it's risky buying a bike you can't at least ride up and down the block a few times. Shopping online on a site like Craigslist is probably the best of both worlds, because you can choose to search for sellers close to you. If you find a great deal, you can arrange to test ride the bike and even take it to a shop to have it checked by a mechanic. It's a much safer approach to buying your first bike than sending off your money and hoping the bike you receive in the mail works out. Plus, if you find a local seller on Craigslist, then you'll be able to avoid shipping costs, too (which can be substantial).

Internet Scams

And as long as we're talking about cautious shopping, it's worth pointing out that there are always scammers out there. Don't feel obligated to follow through with a deal if something doesn't feel right. If you're underage, never give somebody your personal information without letting your parents know you're shopping online. Don't arrange a visit—to your house or a seller's—without going with someone else, or at least telling somebody where you're headed. And while you're at it, don't agree to meet at night. Because who sells bikes at night, anyway?

Bike Swaps

Bike swaps, in addition to being great get-togethers for cyclists, offer deals on everything from kids' bikes to race-ready time-trial bikes. Swaps are worth visiting because you can check out different models in person, bring friends who can help you evaluate gear, and talk to sellers.

Check with local colleges and universities, bike clubs, and on the internet for events. Ask at your local shop, too.

"BOX" STORES

Big "box" stores like Walmart and Target sell a ton of bikes for cheap. Beware, though, because at outlets like these you won't get knowledge-able help, and rock-bottom prices often indicate lower quality. The bikes are often assembled by well-meaning, but inexperienced staff, which can result in poor performance.

AT THE RACES

Occasionally, event organizers will have an "expo area" at bike races, where you'll find people selling old gear. Obviously most of the stuff will be oriented toward racing, but if that's your thing, then you're in luck.

Keep in mind that racers are very hard on their gear, but if something looks well-maintained it's probably all right to buy. You can ask racers, too; most of them are pretty cool and will give you accurate info about how long they've used something or what condition it's in. Just ask.

Between the internet, bike swaps, and your local bike shops, you've got a lot of options. It's probably a good idea to read Chapter 5 on bike fit before you lay down any money. This will help you make an informed choice and get a bike that fits, is comfortable, and works for you.

The International Gold Standard: Doug Emerson and University Bicycles

by Doug Emerson

Choosing a bike shop is like deciding on which dentist or plumber to use. Trust is the main key to the relationship. A simple test to determine the reliability of a bike shop is to ask different employees the same question, such as, "What size bike do you think I need?" You should hear the same answer from each employee. Information should also be consistent from day to day. Getting a different answer on Monday than you heard on Friday is a red flag.

If you are shopping for a new bike, try to check out two or three shops before you buy. You'll probably own your bike for the next ten years, so it's nice to feel comfortable and welcome at the store as many bike shops offer free adjustments for as long as you own your bike. Be sure to ask exactly what "free adjustments" means, and get the full details of the program. "Do I have to make an appointment, or can I just come in for spot adjustments?" (Spontaneous drop-ins should be welcomed.) "Does it include flat-tire repair?" (Probably not.)

Ultimately, you should feel comfortable asking questions, without being made to feel like you're a moron. The best bike shop staff is one that can answer the same question all day long with a smile. There should be no question too simple to answer. (Be aware that bike mechanics are generally a surly bunch, but they tend to cheer up when offered cookies.) When you find a shop with the right vibe, one that you can recommend to your friends, then you're home. Cycling is fun. Pick a fun shop.

Finally, if you are within a hundred miles of University Bicycles in Boulder, I urge you to go there. It is the international gold standard of bike shops.

Doug Emerson opened University Bicycles, in Boulder, Colorado, in 1985. U-Bikes, as it's affectionately known in the community, is now Boulder's oldest shop and one of the most respected and profitable in the United States.

5

FITTING YOUR BIKE

The most important thing to consider when buying a bike—new or used—is fit. The best bike on the planet will be your worst nightmare if it doesn't fit you. After an hour in the saddle you'll be cramped, uncomfortable, and probably annoyed, too. Because you've ridden a bunch of bikes already (right?!), you should have an idea of what feels "right" and what's not going to work.

Getting your bike to fit right can be a complicated project, but don't feel like you've got to nail your bike's position down to the millimeter, or right off the bat. Some riders spend a few months finding their position by trial and error. Some just hop on and go without problems. Others obsess over all the different measurements—saddle height, handlebar height and width, and crank length—and adjust what they feel is "off."

This chapter will give you a great starting point for fitting a road, cyclo-cross, mountain, or touring bike. It's worth taking the time to do it right, too, because changing parts—stems, handlebars, and saddles—can be expensive and time consuming. Keep in mind, too, that everybody's body is different, so what works for most people might not necessarily work for you. So trust yourself; listen to your body.

Whether you're riding to school or work, hopping logs on your mountain bike, or trying out a race, you need to be comfortable—not only for enjoyment, but also for your health. So, if something's aching, tingling, or going numb, don't just tough it out. Fix it!

A CAUTIONARY TALE

The first time I competed in the Colorado state cycling championships, I got a flat tire. I pulled over, waited for the support car to bring me a wheel, and then started chasing the leading group. I hunched over my handlebars and pedaled furiously, but I was alone, without any help. I realized, after a tough ten miles, I wasn't going to catch up with the rest of the gang.

Sitting upright, I rode easily toward the finish, but there was a problem: I couldn't feel my junk. I loved biking, but this was not a price I was willing to pay. I had the evening to ponder my predicament. Needless to say, I did not sleep well that night.

Luckily the numbness eventually went away, and by morning all had returned to normal. (Phew!)

I later found out the problem was my bike's "fit," or the way I had the saddle, stem, and handlebars set up on the frame. Luckily, I happened to live near one of the world's foremost experts on bike fit, Dr. Andy Pruitt. Proper bike fit keeps you healthy, comfortable, and performing your best, and nobody has done more for the science of fit than Dr. Pruitt. I scheduled an appointment.

THE SADDLE

Cyclists call their seat a saddle. Maybe it's because the first bicycle seats were unpadded leather, just like horse saddles. What's more important than why we call them saddles is how much more comfortable they are today than they were twenty-five years ago. They're only comfy, though, if they're positioned properly, so let's cover some basic anatomy, and then work on getting your saddle right where it needs to be.

Saddle Up!

LOVE YOUR BUTT

One of the most common complaints in cycling is what is oh-so-techni-cally known as a "pain in the butt." Your butt does some very important things, so you'd better keep it happy. Turns out it has a few important neighbors, too.

There are a bunch of nerves and blood vessels supplying oxygen and sensation to your equipment down there, and they run through the area on which you sit when cycling. If your weight rests too far forward, rather than sitting on the two pointy "sit bones" under your butt, you can decrease the blood supply or compress a nerve—and that means numb junk. Girls can experience tingling, burning, or numbness. Boys can, too, but they can also damage veins and arteries, which can lead to other more serious problems. In stark terms, that's your basic nightmare scenario. Bike fit is starting to sound important, right?

Cop Comfort

Maybe you've seen your friendly neighborhood police offi-cer pedaling his or her bike while on patrol. It seems like the best assignment you could get as a cop. Bike police have also been instrumental in helping design better, more comfortable saddles. They spend hours on the bike, every day, so who better to help? Several brands have designed saddles using the data gleaned from bike cops. Who knew?

Spending a few extra bucks on a saddle is well worth it. The more com-fortable you are, the longer you'll be able to ride (and faster, too). Really good shops often have several models you can borrow and ride for a bit, before making a decision to buy. Tell the staff what kind of riding you'll be doing, too, because different models work better for different types of cycling. If your shop can't loan you a saddle, then ride your friends' bikes and see what feels good. Whatever you do, don't just buy what looks cool—get what fits and what feels right.

DETERMINING YOUR SADDLE HEIGHT

Saddle height is the most obvious element of bike fit. Raise your saddle and your legs get straighter while pedaling; lower it and your legs are more bent at the bottom of their pedal stroke.

Here's a way to get a pretty good idea of your ideal saddle height for road, 'cross, touring, commuting, and mountain biking. (For trials, jumping, and BMX, your saddle height is more a matter of personal preference, so these rules don't apply.)

For starters, you'll need a friend, your cycling shorts (or the shorts you ride in), a straight edge (a ruler, carpenter's square, or even a large book), measuring tape, a pencil, and a calculator (unless you're a math genius).

Wear your shorts and stand barefoot against a wall, facing out, with your feet normally spaced—not too wide and not together. Put your ruler (or substitute) firmly against your crotch with medium pressure, touching the wall behind you. Have your friend mark where the ruler contacts the wall.

Now, take the measurement from your crotch to the floor in centimeters and multiply it by .883. A French cycling coach in the '70s and '80s arrived at .883 as the appropriate multiplier to determine most riders'

TRICKS OF THE TRADE

A Quick Cure for Knee Pain

Knee pain is a common cycling complaint. As a very rough rule, pain in the front of the knee is generally from too low of a saddle, while pain in the back of the knee is associated with too high of a saddle. If your knees hurt, raise or lower your saddle a few millimeters (depending on where the pain is), and see if it helps.

saddle heights. Current medical professionals like Dr. Pruitt have verified its applicability to most cyclists. So if your measurement is 90 centimeters, you'd take multiple 90 by .883 to get 79.5 centimeters. (If you did that in your head, then congratulations! You have a bright future counting cards in Vegas.) This number is your saddle height, measuring from the center of your bottom-bracket axle to the top of your saddle, staying in line with your seat tube. If you ever borrow a bike, get a new one, or rent one, you can use this number to set the saddle height at the right position—no guessing and way less trial and error. This is an old-school method (newer methods employ a protractor-like device to measure the angle of your knee while on the bike), but it should get you pretty close to your ideal height. As with any fit advice or formulas, your comfort trumps everything. If something hurts, then make adjustments!

SADDLE POSITIONING: NOT TOO FORE, NOT TOO AFT

Now that you're sitting at the right height, we need to slide your saddle forward or backward—fore or aft, in bike-geek speak. Finding the sweet spot helps you pedal more efficiently, but also reduces pressure on your hands and protects your back.

Get a piece of string and tie something relatively heavy, like a wrench or a big nut, to the end of it. Get comfortable on your bike, in your most "natural" riding position, and then hold the end of the string against the front of your kneecap. Position your leg so your bike's crankarm (the aluminum bar connecting the pedal to the frame's bottom bracket) is parallel to the ground (your foot will be in the three o'clock position when viewed from the right).

Once your leg hits "three," have a buddy eyeball you from the side to confirm that your crank is parallel to the ground. Your string, with your heavy object hanging below your foot, should just touch the end of your crankarm. If your string is not touching the tip of the crankarm, loosen the bolts on your seatpost's clamp to allow you to slide your saddle forward or backward to get your string in the right spot.

Your saddle should now be properly adjusted! It should also be "flat," and not tipped up or down. If you're having to tip your saddle up or down, it can be an indication of other fit problems.

HANDLEBAR POSITION

There's no set formula for bike fit, particularly when it comes to handlebar position. Between the handlebars and the stem, there are a million different combinations. You can buy stems and bars in lots of different heights and widths, so you should be able to get comfortable with the help of a shop, or just by trial and error.

When you're starting out, don't try to look like the Tour de France guys—their bodies have spent years adapting to racing, so they can do things you and I can't. The main issues here are comfort and bike handling, so

TRICKS OF THE TRADE

How to Fit a Helmet

Don't overlook proper fit for your helmet either. An ill-fitting helmet won't protect your head and face in a crash, so make sure you've got the right size and it's adjusted to fit you.

First, try on a few helmets—like shoes, each model has a slightly different shape, so go with one that's comfortable. Once on, leave the helmet's chin strap unbuckled and shake your head side-to-side. The helmet shouldn't slide around, fly off your noggin, or slip too far forward or back. If it has an adjustable band within the helmet, make sure it's comfortably snug. Now buckle the chin strap so it gently contacts your chin.

The front of your helmet should sit just above your eyebrows, not have any pressure points, and should be replaced every three to four years. Consult the owner's manual to make sure you're set up correctly—and enjoy!

don't settle for a position that doesn't feel right or makes it hard to control your bike.

There are a bunch of ways to determine handlebar position, but roughly speaking you want to have a gentle forward bend at the waist and a comfortable bend in the elbows when sitting on the saddle and resting your hands in your preferred riding position (usually atop the brakes on a road or 'cross bike; on the grips on a mountain bike). Typically you're more upright on a mountain bike and bent a bit more forward on a road bike.

The following method is a bit old-school—meaning it was developed for wool-clad road cyclists—but it still works. If you're fitting your mountain bike, keep in mind that your bars will be higher and a couple centimeters closer to you than this method indicates. BMX is a whole different ball game—because you sit so much lower on your saddle—so, for BMX fit, let comfort and bike handling guide you, more than any set formula.

Put your elbow against the tip (or "nose") of the saddle, then reach your arm toward the handlebars. The tips of your fingers should almost reach the part of the stem where the handlebars connect. Your bars should be just about level or slightly below the tip of your saddle on a road bike and closer to level on a mountain bike. Start with these ideas as a guide, see how it feels, and I bet you'll be close to your "ideal" position.

FEET AND CLEATS

We've talked about your butt, your hands, and even your "junk." Your feet are feeling left out right about now.

Why are feet important? Because pedaling a bike is such a repetitive motion. If your pedal, cleat, or shoe position is out of whack, it can lead to knee pain, back problems, or other issues.

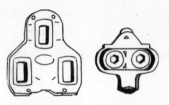

Lots of people start cycling with plain street shoes and "toe clips," or the straps that cover the top of your feet and connect you to the pedals. These are fine for

Road Cleat   Moutain Cleat

riding to and from school or work, or if you're just starting out in cycling, but if you'll be riding a lot, cycling shoes with cleats and "clipless" pedals are the way to go—they're more efficient and they're safer, too.

Besides a good saddle, putting a little extra money into cycling-specific shoes is probably the smartest thing you can do for your comfort. Cycling shoes come predrilled for cleats, which fit into your pedals (much like a ski boot fits into a ski binding). Most types of pedals require their own proprietary cleats. Almost all of the popular pedal brands are strong, lightweight, and are great options, so don't stress about what kind to get, just make sure you have the proper cleats.

"You don't need to spend $300," explains Pruitt. "One-hundred dollar shoes are fine, but make it a cycling-specific shoe. Low-end mountain bike shoes are great."

Once you have your shoes, you'll need to mount and position your cleats on the soles. Hop up on a table and let your legs hang off the end, as if you're sitting on a dock, dangling your feet in the water. Notice how your feet hang. Are they turned way out (duck-footed)? Turned in (pigeon-toed)? Some riders are even pigeon-toed on one side and duck-footed on the other, which makes things even more interesting!

Keep your natural foot position in mind when bolting the cleats onto the bottom of your shoes. Start by positioning the cleat so that the axle of the pedal runs beneath the ball of your foot. Depending on the position of your feet—do they turn in or out, or are they neutral?—you can rotate your cleat a millimeter or two to allow for the most natural pedaling position. Once you start riding, you'll be able to feel whether your cleats are aligned or not. During your first few rides you can take an Allen wrench along so you can make adjustments along the way.

Still not comfortable? Some of us have one leg longer than the other, or long legs with a short upper body, or tight hamstrings, and so on. These peculiarities sometimes make getting comfortable on the bike more difficult. If you've tinkered with your position and you're still uncomfortable, then visit your bike shop and ask about getting a professional fit. The person doing it should measure your legs and eyeball the rest of your body for anything that you might've missed. If the person doesn't go over your riding style and give your bod a good check, then use another shop. Stick with it, and don't settle for anything less than total comfort!

Fit Means Bike Fun

By Andy Pruitt and Rob Coppolillo

"Young riders gotta have fun, and being uncomfortable isn't fun," says Pruitt. Our goal here, until you make it to the Tour de France and start earning the big bucks, is that you have a good time. If you're smiling, then you'll ride more, and riding more will make you a better cyclist. That's our formula for success.

When starting out, "Get a bike you can grow into," Pruitt advises. And if you're buying a used bike, "Remember, you are buying somebody else's position. Most folks don't take care of their bikes for resale."

What Pruitt means by this is that certain adjustments on a bike are impossible if the previous owner didn't plan for it. For example, raising the handlebars by moving the stem higher on the fork's steerer tube won't work if the owner cut the steerer tube down so it's flush with the top of the stem. Professionals often do this to save weight, but keep in mind that if you're buying a bike and need to raise the bars, you'll need to have some steerer tube showing above the stem. Many bikes don't have that.

If you're buying new, then make sure you buy what works and not what's cool. And most important, "Fit the bike to the rider, not the rider to the bike," explains Dr. Pruitt. Bicycle frames all have slightly different dimensions, so make sure you get one that will accommodate your own particular needs. Again, a good bike shop will help.

When purchasing your bike, new or used, Pruitt says, "Buy a bike to grow with. Start with it a little big." There are several ways to do this, he explains—by buying the next-larger frame size and by leaving the steerer tube a bit long.

"Too often as a kid grows," he says, "they just raise the saddle without raising their handlebar position. Eventually their fit is off, and compromises in fit become handling issues." Leaving the steerer long will allow you to raise your handlebars as you grow taller while preserving your bike's handling.

With a little planning, you can get yourself onto a bike that will fit perfectly. Make a smart purchase, and then spend an afternoon fine-tuning your position. You'll feel better, ride faster, and your bike will handle like a dream.

We'll get to a more thorough discussion of fit in the next chapter, but in the meantime, here are some things to keep in mind:

- Raising the saddle/seat post is easy, but adding height to the stem and handlebars requires at least a new stem, if not length on the fork's steerer tube (the part that comes up and out of the front, into your bike's frame). Make sure you can get the handlebars in a comfortable position.
- If you're still growing, err on the side of buying your bike slightly big, so you'll grow into it.
- Consider women's brake levers for road and 'cross bikes; they're easier to reach for almost everybody but fully grown men.
- Saddles are like shoes—go with what fits your body, not what looks cool.

_____

Dr. Pruitt began as an athletic trainer at the University of Colorado before working for the US Cycling Federation, and later, founding his own clinic, The Boulder Center for Sports Medicine in Boulder, Colorado. Through his twenties he also became a top-level amateur cyclist, despite having lost his lower right leg in a childhood hunting accident. He won two national and two world championships racing with a prosthetic limb. Today, the best athletes in the world come to his clinic for help with injuries, bike fit, and training. Dr. Pruitt has a doctorate in education, holds a physicians assistant degree, and is also the author of Andy Pruitt's Complete Medical Guide for Cyclists *(add it to your library!), the definitive book on fit and medical issues for cyclists.*

6

KEEPING IT ROLLING

Ah, the fine art of bicycle maintenance. Keeping your bike in good working order requires equal parts skill and patience. With just a little coaching, you can master the skills necessary to fix common problems with your bike. As for patience, I encourage you to channel the calm mind of a Zen monk, and don't rush the job. Bikes aren't all that complicated when you break them down, so if you take a little time to do it right, you should get the results you're looking for.

Do-it-yourself (DIY) maintenance will save you cash and head off problems before they turn into mechanical nightmares. Besides that, it's also really interesting. Figuring out how to adjust a headset won't take you long, and you'll be psyched when you can fine-tune yours to perfection. Study the following material, and you'll be well on your way to being a self-sufficient bike mechanic.

RULES TO WRENCH BY

Before you roll up the sleeves, bust out the tools, and get down to "wrenching," let's establish some ground rules.

Though you obviously possess the strength of ten Clydesdale horses, try not to overdo it. Any time something feels stuck, blocked, or otherwise uncooperative, resist the urge to overpower it with your fearsome musculature. Instead, take a good look at the part or situation, and see if you're missing something. Is it rusted and therefore seized up? Did you loosen all the bolts? Are you truly loosening it, rather than accidentally tightening it? Remember, some parts, like the left pedal on a bike, are "reverse threaded," meaning that they tighten to the left, not the right.

Now that you're working with a calm mind and soft touch, take a moment to assess your project. Is it within your capabilities? Can you figure it out on your own? Sometimes it's fun to tinker a bit and see what you can do, but certain things—suspension forks, for example—don't really lend themselves to novice DIY adventures. For projects that seem too complicated, don't hesitate to ask your local shop for advice, search the internet for info and video tutorials, or consult a repair book.

Where to Get Help

Before you jump down the rabbit hole, do some research on the maintenance or repair you're performing. The League of American Bicyclists (bikeleague.org) has online help for common stuff, as does About.com (bicycling.about.com). The popular Zinn guides cover just about every repair you'll encounter. Find them at your local shop or online at VeloPress.com.

A lot of bicycle repair depends on the tools you have. Removing rear cogs or disassembling a bottom bracket (refer to the biking diagram on page 8 if you're not sure where to find these parts) requires simple but specialized tools. Don't try to improvise: either spend the money for the right tool, or have a shop mechanic do the work. You'll save yourself a load of frustration, and you'll be less likely to damage your bike.

GETTING DIRTY

We're about to get down to the most common repairs, so jump into your coveralls and prepare to get dirty. Some of these repairs are actually routine maintenance you should do periodically (like lubing the chain), while others are "on-the-fly"—stuff that will come up during a ride. If you find yourself having fun working on your bike, then consider asking at your shop about a job. Why not make a little cash for your hard efforts?

TIRE MAINTENANCE

Your tires are your connection to the world, so you've got to keep them happy. Check them occasionally for cracks, embedded junk from the road, or just plain old wear and tear. A recommended pressure is printed on the side of the tire, and you should generally keep your tires within this range. You'll flat less, your tires will last longer, and your bike will handle better.

Check the tire pressure every few days. A good floor pump, a pump designed for use at home or in a shop, will usually have a pressure gauge on it. Hook it up to your tire's valve, pump a couple times and you'll see how many PSIs (pounds per square inch) you have. If your tires are overinflated, simply detach the pump, press the valve head with your fingernail, and let out a little air. Now you're ready to roll.

Fixing a Flat

The most common bike problem is the flat tire. Glass, tiny pebbles, or occasionally an errant shard of metal can all puncture your tire and the tube that lies within it—and then you're on the hook to either call for a ride or fix it yourself. With a little practice, you'll be able to fix a flat in three minutes or less—no need to let it ruin your day. To fix a flat, whether you're riding or at home, you'll need a spare inner-tube, a pump, tire levers, and maybe a patch kit.

With a flat rear tire, you'll notice a squishy, bouncing feeling from the back end of your bike. If you happen to flat your front tire, you'll probably notice it more quickly (wobbly steering and poor handling offer clear warning signs that you're losing air). In either event, pull over, because if your tube goes completely flat inside its tire, the whole enchilada can roll off the rim and cause you to crash (and you'll damage the wheel, too!).

If you do get a flat, hop off your bike and move somewhere safe, out of the way of other bike traffic. To fix the flat, you'll need to take the entire wheel off the bike. Road, mountain, 'cross, some town bikes, and many fixies have "quick-release" levers that attach the wheel to the bike. These are simple to use; just pull the lever open, and the wheel should drop out of the fork or frame. If you're riding without quick-release levers—on a BMX bike, for example—then you'll need a wrench or two to loosen the nuts on the wheel.

The Basics of Pumping

Most pumps, whether they're compact versions designed to bring along on a ride or full-sized models ("floor pumps") to be used at home, function similarly. One end slides over the air valve on your wheel and then you grab the handle and pump air steadily into the tube. Usually there is a lever that flips up and locks the pump onto the valve, keeping it sealed while you pump.

There are two types of valves—"Presta" and "Schrader." The larger, more common ones (especially on cars) are Schraders, while the skinnier ones (found on mountain and road bikes, usually) are Prestas.

Larger pumps for use at home or in a bike shop generally have a pressure gauge, while compact ones do not. If you're on a ride and need to pump up a flat, just use your hand to gauge how much air to put in by squeezing the tire on your other wheel, or on a friend's bike.

Once you have the wheel off, peel the tire off the rim using your hands. If that's too difficult, use a tire lever—a plastic lever that will help you pry the edge of the tire over the rim. Once the tire is off, pull the tube from within it. Often you can see the hole already, but if not, pump some air into the tube. Hear a hissing sound? Find it and there's your hole.

Before you put a new tube in the tire, run your fingers along the inside of the tire and make sure whatever punctured your tire isn't still there. A common mistake is to put a new tube in the tire, pump it up, and bang—it goes flat again because a chunk of glass was still embedded in the tire. Woops!

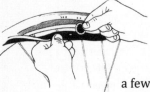

If you have a patch kit, you can patch the hole, provided it's small enough. Without a patch kit, you'll need a spare tube. In either case, take the repaired/new tube and put just a few pumps of air into it (this will make it easier to get inside the tire and back on the rim). Put the tube inside your tire and then put one side of the tire onto the rim, slowly working it around the rest of the rim. Next, pop the other side of the tire on. It's best if you can do it with your hands, but if not, use the tire lever to force the edge (or "bead") of the tire back onto the rim. Be careful if

TRICKS OF THE TRADE

The Power of the Patch

Tiny patch kits are inexpensive and easy to use. Simply clean the area around the hole on your tube, peel the backing off the patch, and stick the patch over the hole. Press with your hands for a few seconds and *voilà*, good as new.

using a lever, because you can pinch the inner-tube between the lever and rim, which can put a hole in the tube, putting you back at square one.

Once the tire and tube are back on the rim, inflate the tube with your pump. Put in about ten strokes with your pump, then let out all the air and start over. This helps seat the tire and tube on the rim, so nothing gets pinched and punctured again. Pump up to your desired hardness (feeling with your hands or a pressure gauge), then put the wheel back in the fork or frame. Make absolutely sure the quick-release, or wheel nuts, are tightened properly before riding. If the wheel flies out while you're hitting mach speeds, it won't be a pretty sight.

GET RID OF THE SQUEAK—CARING FOR YOUR CHAIN

Does it sound like you have a family of mice living in your backpack when you pedal home? It's probably just your chain, begging for the tender loving care that only you can provide.

To take good care of your chain, you'll need some old rags or paper towels, a good solvent or citrus degreaser, and some chain lube. Some companies make little contraptions especially for chain cleaning, but don't feel like you've got to have one to get your lube on.

Start by spraying down your chain with the solvent. This will dissolve old lubricant and help work dirt out of the links. Let it sit for 18 minutes. Remember, you have the patience of a Zen monk, so this should be easy. Next, wipe down the chain with rags, trying to get all the solvent and goop off. An old toothbrush can help if you're working with a super-dirty chain. (Hot tip: Don't reuse the greasy toothbrush.)

Once the chain is sparkly clean, apply the lube, following the instructions on the bottle. Now let it set again for a few minutes. You can spin the pedals backward to help the new lubricant really work into the pins and links of the chain. After a few minutes, wipe down the chain to remove any excess lube, as it will only attract dirt. Repeat every few days or as soon as you start hearing those mice again.

Threaded Versus Threadless

Older headsets screw onto the fork's steerer tube, which is threaded to accept a locking ring. These adjust differently than modern "threadless" systems, but are pretty rare these days. Ask for help at your shop or look online if you pick up a bike with this kind of headset.

HEADS UP FOR A SOLID HEADSET

Your bike's handlebars connect to its stem. The stem clamps around the top of the fork's steerer tube, and this allows you to turn the front wheel.

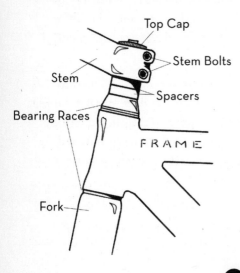

Top Cap

Stem Bolts

Stem

Spacers

Bearing Races

FRAME

Fork

Simple, right? Not so fast; integral to this whole system are the bearings within your "headset."

Headsets are the bearings and nuts that allow your handlebars to turn smoothly. You'll never notice them when they're adjusted properly, but just a millimeter of "play," or looseness, and you'll feel it every time you hit a bump in the road. It will drive you nuts! Here's how to adjust a "threadless" headset.

If you feel a little rattle (or "play") in your headset, verify that it's your headset that's loose (and not something else) by pulling your front brake firmly with your right hand, then rocking the bike forward and back. While you're doing this, grasp the headset where it attaches to the steerer tube (on top of the frame's head tube) and feel for play. Not loose? Check your brakes and front hub for adjustment problems.

If you need to tighten up the headset, start by loosening the two stem bolts (these are at the end of the stem closest to the frame; they clamp around the fork's steerer tube). Once these are loose, tighten the single bolt on top of the stem—the one you look down on when you're riding. It pulls the top of the stem down and compresses the bearings into adjustment. Do this in quarter-turn increments and recheck after each quarter-turn.

Take your time. Once there's no more play in the headset, retighten the two stem bolts that clamp the steerer tube. Now, lift the front wheel of your bike up by the handlebars and tilt the wheel side to side. Does your front wheel gradually fall toward the tilt? If it's locked up and won't turn on its own, then your headset is too tight. If it rotates smoothly, then you, my friend, have just adjusted your headset. My compliments, and enjoy your plush ride.

OH-SO-SWEET SHIFTING

For any bike with cables—shifting or braking—the best thing you can do for performance is frequent lubrication. Cables eventually get dry within the plastic "housing" that surrounds them. Once dry, they create friction making it difficult to shift and brake. With ten minutes of attention and a little lube, your bike will run like new again.

Here's a little trick to lubricating your bike's cables. Put the rear wheel into its largest cog by shifting the derailleur while pedaling the bike. You can do this while riding, or by lifting the bike with one hand while alternating shifting and pedaling with the other. Once the chain is on the largest cog, dismount, or just stop the rear wheel from rolling (if you're pedaling it by hand). Now, shift the rear derailleur a few clicks toward its lower (shorter, or more-difficult-to-pedal) gears, without turning the cranks.

Now check out the rear wheel. See how the derailleur tried to jump down a few gears? Because we didn't pedal the cranks and move the chain, the derailleur cable has slack in it, which will allow us to get at it and lubricate it. Take the cable and its plastic housing and pop it out of the little guides on the frame. Slide the housing up the cable and expose the part that's normally hidden. Put a drop of lube on that section and smooth it around with your fingertips. Do this for any section you can access by sliding the plastic housing up and down.

When you're finished lubing, reposition the cables and housing in their proper spots and slot them into the guides on the frame. Pedal the bike a few turns and the derailleur will jump back into position—and your shifting should be way smoother than before.

Repeat the process with your front derailleur, but this time shift it onto its largest chainring (on the outside) while pedaling the bike. Notice how the derailleur cable is now tight? Perform the same trick as with the rear derailleur: Without pedaling, shift the front derailleur as if you're going to the smaller, easier chainrings. Your front derailleur cable should now have slack in it, just like your rear did.

Bike Chain Tool

Slide the housing and cable down to expose the area that's usually covered, lube it, and then pop the cable and housing back into place. That's all it takes!

Repair Kits

If you're going to be riding far and wide, you should always carry a miniature repair kit with you. A basic kit includes a micro-pump, patch kit, spare tube, a master link for your chain, and a multi-tool. The multi-tool can be as large or as small as you like, but at a minimum you should probably have a chain tool, a few Allen wrenches, a couple screwdrivers, and a couple sizes of spoke wrenches. With this you can perform the most common roadside repairs, and the whole kit is about the size of a good hunk of banana bread.

SHOCK AND AWE: MAINTAINING YOUR SUSPENSION

All right, for you mountain bikers, it's time to take a quick look at your suspension. Most mountain bikes these days have at least front suspension forks, while a full suspension bike will also offer a rear shock integrated with the frame. Both of these require some regular maintenance to keep you and your bike happy.

Forks come in so many different configurations that you'll want to consult an online video tutorial or get an in-depth book if you're looking to do much more than basic adjustments. For day-to-day riding, though, you need to at least maintain your air pressure and check for blown seals.

Most shocks, front and rear, have an air chamber or two that you can adjust based upon your weight and riding style. Nobody wants to hear that they have to "consult your owner's manual," but in this case it's pretty unavoidable. Keeping your suspension adjusted properly will improve your handling and make your riding way more comfortable. It's worth the time. Check for an online version of your manual if you don't have the printed one.

First, check the manual to see where you need to add air, keeping in mind that there may be two places to adjust pressure. Your fork should come with a shock pump, which is just a mini bike pump with a special attachment for your shock. The pump will have a pressure gauge on it, and a little flexible tube that screws onto your fork's air valve. Your manual should show you how and where, as well as give you a chart with recommended pressure for your body weight. You can go a little harder if you like a firmer ride, or slightly softer if you like a plush, softer feeling to your bike. Experiment, but stay pretty close to the recommended pressure.

Keep Your Oil Where it Belongs—Inside Your Shocks

Most suspension systems, front and rear, contain lubricating oil. The oil keeps parts moving well and also provides some resistance in combination with the air pressure. Tiny seals keep the oil inside the shock where it belongs, and you should check these after every few rides. You'll see that on most shocks, both front and rear, there's a smooth rod that pushes into the shock when it's compressed. Your seals hug this rod, keeping dirt and debris out of the guts of the shock and protecting the oil inside. If there's more than a thin film of oil on this rod, you may have a leak. Have your shop look at it sooner rather than later and replace seals as necessary. It will cost you a bit (usually around $100), but it will also extend the life of your fork.

RANDOM ACTS OF SQUEAKINESS

Despite your best efforts to maintain a spotless and perfectly tuned machine, some things will eventually get out of whack. Usually it's easy to identify what's broken or in need of adjustment, but occasionally you'll develop a mystery click, clack, squeak, or creak. So, then what? Included below are some essential trouble-shooting techniques for the most common problems.

Unholy Spokes: Wheel Drama

Between your front and rear wheels combined, you have a few dozen spokes along for the ride. Notice how they screw into "nipples" along the rims and then hook through your hubs at the opposite ends. When your wheels were built, a skilled mechanic (that, or an expensive machine in Taiwan or China) carefully tensioned them between the hub and rim. This keeps your wheel round and "true"—or without side-to-side wobbles when viewed from above—but keep in mind the spokes are actively pulling on the rim. Your wheel exists in balance between all these spokes pulling opposite each other.

In general, spoked wheels work really well, but after a few potholes, a couple of rough roads, and that monster air you launched last weekend, they can develop problems. A symptom of problems can be loose spokes. Spokes can even break (you'll hear a loud ping!), but usually before they do you'll get some metallic creaking. If you hear this creaking, stop and flex each of your spokes with your hand. Do they feel tensioned equally? Keep in mind that your front wheel should feel equally tensioned on both sides, while your rear wheel's right side, or "drive" side (the side with the gears on it), spokes will be tighter than those on the left, or non-"drive" side.

If you discover a few loose spokes or several that seem overtightened, take your wheels down to your shop and ask the mechanics to "true" them and check for "roundness." If you've developed a good relationship with your shop, maybe you can ask them to show you basic truing. It's not too hard to correct minor problems; you'll just need a spoke wrench to start.

The Tick-Tick of a Derailleur Cable

Another sneaky problem can be your derailleur cables, particularly in the front. Notice that there's an extra inch of cable coming through the derailleur. It's where the mechanic cut it off when assembling your bike. If this bit becomes bent, the end of your crankarm can hit it every time you pedal. (Tick, tick, tick.) Don't forget to check it!

Ker-Chunk! (How to Pack a Saddle Bag)

If you ride with a seat pack, then take a second to arrange the items within it. Put your metal stuff in the lower portion of the pack and put the tube on top of those, so when you hit a bump the tube will keep the metal stuff from bouncing against your saddle. You'll have a quieter ride and you won't get a loud ker-chunk when you hop a curb or cross some railroad tracks.

A QUICK WORD ABOUT SAFETY

Back in the olden days, riders carried a quarter with them at all times, so that they'd always be able to call someone from a pay phone if they had an irreparable mechanical problem and ended up stranded. Today we have the cheap and easy cell phone—a vast improvement over the quarter and corner phone option—which should be a mandatory accessory

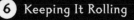

for any ride (especially since pay phones barely exist these days!). It's never a good idea to resort to hitchhiking or catching a ride with someone creepy. And remember to let somebody know where you're headed on your two-wheeled ad ventures. Enjoy!

Downloadable Bonus Content

Download fix-it tips and tricks to your smart phone while on your ride at zestbooks.net/holy-spokes-bonus. Keep the PDF on your smart phone so that you are always ready for any emergency fix-it situation.

Quick Fixes on the Road

By Brady Kappius

Rear Derailleur

It's one of the most annoying things when you're out for a ride and your bike won't stay in the right gear. It's usually a really simple fix, requiring just the twist of a screw.

The first step is to figure out which way the chain is trying to go. Is it trying to fall down (to a smaller cog and a more difficult gear) the rear cogs, or go up them? If it's going down, your tension needs tightening. To do this, go to either your shifter or rear derailleur. You will find a "barrel adjuster" where the cable comes out of the shifter or goes into the derailleur.

Now, imagine looking down the housing (the plastic that covers the cable) and into the shifter, or at the other end of the cable into the derailleur and twisting the barrel counter-clockwise. This will tighten the cable and bring the derailleur back up the cogs. Chain trying to go up the cassette? Just rotate the barrel adjuster clockwise to decrease the tension.

Try a half-turn in the direction you think you need, then pedal for a bit and see if it's helped.

Chain Repair

Chain breakage is a less common occurrence, but when it happens, you will be happy that you know how to repair it. You will need two items: a chain tool and a master link. You should always carry a multi-tool, with a chain tool, in your seat bag, along with a master link. These are items you can get at any bike shop for next to nothing. Just make sure you get the type that matches the width of your chain (8-, 9-,10-or 11-speed).

To fix the chain, use your tool to press out the damaged link(s). Any that are bent or broken need to be removed. The chain needs to have only inner plates showing, so make sure you press them out so that the narrow part of the chain is the half left exposed on both sides. Then take your master link and put it through the two halves of the chain, turn the cranks so that the master link is on the top section of the chain, between the cogs and cranks. Now crank the pedals with your hand. The master link will pop into position and you will be ready to go.

If you removed several damaged links, remember the chain is now a lot shorter. Be careful if you ride in the big ring and in the large rear cog, because the chain could be too short. If so, replace with a new chain when you make it back home.

Badly Bent Wheel

Sometimes when out on the mountain bike you might go a little too big, land wrong, and "taco" a wheel (bending it like a taco).

Don't fret! There is still hope of getting home. All you need is a rock (or even just a solid patch of earth) and some arm power. Determine the part of the wheel most out of true (that is, most bent) and give it a big whack. Do this until the wheel will spin in the frame freely. You might have to disconnect your brake (don't forget and go bombing down the hills!), but at least you can slowly ride home. The rim and spokes will be trashed, but you'll make it home for dinner, instead of calling for help.

Brady Kappius is a member of Team Clif Bar, the nation's strongest youth cyclo-cross team. He competes throughout the United States and is a future World Cup rider.

7

STAYING SAFE

Making the bike a daily part of your life means you'll be spending a lot of time on two wheels (probably amongst traffic and the chaos of urbanized life). Staying healthy, saving money, and helping Mother Earth are admirable reasons for riding, but none of them mean very much if you get pancaked while cycling. Here are a few tips to keep you in one piece and smiling.

There are also some good apps for smartphones that will help you navigate through cities, and even browse other riders' routes. You can also visit BicyclingInfo.org and use their nationwide map-finding tool for regional and city maps. Do a little digging and map out a few rides around town. You'll be safer and you'll enjoy it more.

SAFETY GEAR

Above all else—and it's worth repeating here—keep your brain safe by wearing a helmet, and keep your body safe by using your brain. Pay attention to cars coming toward you and entering your line of travel from side streets. Riding while listening to your iPod is tempting—and I'll admit I've done it—but on streets with traffic, it's a bad idea. Try not to, or at least leave the volume low enough to hear yourself shift. That way you'll definitely hear cars approaching.

If you're riding much, eventually you'll be pedaling home in the dark. Most cities and states have laws that require you to have a front and rear light, but even if your state doesn't—do it anyway! You've got to be visible, so a flashing red light in the rear and a white front headlight (often flashing) will help a lot. Reflective stickers on your bike make you a bit more visible, too. You can buy these at bike shops, hardware stores, or online.

If you live in a rainy place like Seattle, then fenders are a good idea. They're not necessarily a safety item, but they will make riding in the rain way more tolerable. The wheels on a bike spray gallons of water upward when turning on a sodden road, and fenders will keep you drier. A good rain jacket, preferably in a bright color for visibility, will help, too.

TRICKS OF THE TRADE

Riding Safe: Traffic Laws

State laws give cyclists the same rights and obligations as cars, which means you can ride on most streets and roads (unless specifically designated as nonbike routes), but you're expected to obey the same laws as cars—stop at red lights and stop signs, signal your turns (left arm straight out for a left turn, or out and up, bent at the elbow, for a right turn), yield to pedestrians in crosswalks, etc. Pay attention to traffic laws, and you'll be safer and more courteous, too.

THE BEST WAYS NOT TO CRASH

By now, the bike is your preferred mode of transportation for local trips. You know where to ride and you're the model of safety. Now the trick is keeping the rubber on the road—that is, not crashing. Here are a few quick ways to keep you upright and smiling.

Look Out for Obstacles

Any object on the road—train tracks, a seam in the pavement, a curb into a parking lot—that runs parallel to your wheels is potentially dangerous. When you need to cross over something (train tracks, usually) cross as close to a right angle as possible. When any object runs parallel to you, your tires will tend to slide along it, rather than roll over it, so watch out for curbs, grooves, or anything that might catch your wheels.

Instead of looking down at your front wheel while riding, scan the road ahead for potholes, rocks, glass, or anything that might cause you to crash or give you a flat. That said, don't swerve into car traffic to avoid an obstacle. If there's something big enough to knock you off your bike, slow down and get around it safely on the shoulder or even on the sidewalk. If you're on the sidewalk, give pedestrians the right of way. In some states, cycling on a sidewalk is actually illegal, so be cool. No dive-bombing a grandma!

Don't Get Doored

Getting doored happens when a person in a parked car opens his or her door into you and it's a real threat—especially in cities. Bike messengers call this being "doored," and you can get seriously injured if you're on the losing end of a collision. If you're riding alongside a line of parked cars, pay attention, as drivers will sometimes open their doors into your lane. Try to look into cars to see if there's a driver sitting there. If there is, watch out for him or her exiting. Sometimes you can see drivers in their rearview mirrors. Pay attention and be ready to stop or go around if the traffic behind you permits.

If you do happen to get doored, in most states this is the driver's fault. Do not let the motorist blame you and leave the scene. If you are injured or your bike is damaged, politely tell the motorist you need to call the police and file a report. If the person leaves, get his or her license plate and a description of the driver. The law varies from state to state, but you should always call the police when you have a crash like this. Keep in mind, too, that you might be injured and not know it, as there's often a rush of adrenaline after an accident that can mask your injuries.

Don't Get KO'd by the Right Hook

Another all-too-common car hazard is the infamous "right hook." This happens when a car passes you on your left and then makes a right turn in front of you. Cars sometimes don't realize you're moving almost as fast as they are, so often when they pass and then slow down to make a right, they forget you're still pretty close behind. If a car passes and slows, assume it's about to turn in front of you—slow down, check for its blinker, and be prepared to hit your brakes.

How to Handle a Crash

If you ride enough, eventually you'll hit the deck. But don't worry, most bike crashes involve only scrapes and some lost skin. The most important thing after a crash is making sure you're safe, so if you're at the side of the road, in the middle of the trail, or on a bike path, get your bod and bike out of traffic, and assess your damage. Ride home if you're able, but if not, don't hesitate to call for help. Once home, clean out your cuts and "road rash," and then apply a sterile, nonstick dressing on top, or a breathable membrane-like patch works well, too. And remember, if you think you're seriously hurt, or any time you hit your head, err on the side of caution and dial 911!

No Swearing, People!

Eventually a car is going to pull a bonehead maneuver and maybe even cause you to swerve or stop. It's really easy to let your temper flare and yell at a driver—but try not to. Why? First, most drivers are just doing their thing, like you. They're trying to get the bills paid, pick up the kids, make it home safely. Chances are the driver is just a nice person making an honest mistake. Second, there's too much road rage out there these days. I've had buddies get pepper-sprayed or threatened by angry motorists. It doesn't happen often, but it does happen, so don't provoke anybody. Keeping your cool also helps you make better decisions in the moment.

If a driver does harass or threaten you, get a license plate and a description of the driver. Have your police department's nonemergency number and your county sheriff's department programmed into your phone. Remember the license plate number and call it in. Even if the police don't find the driver this time, they'll have a complaint about his or her license on record, which will be important if he or she is involved in a similar situation down the road.

SAVING THE PLANET

Bicycling offers a million fun and healthy experiences for us cyclists, but it's also one of the best things we can do for old Mother Earth, too. Most scientists seem to think the world is warming up due to climate change, so using the bike for transportation and as a relatively green recreational activity are great ways to lessen our environmental impact.

For much of the world, the bike is the cheapest, easiest, and most reliable transportation there is. In places like Tanzania, Bolivia, and China, you'll see people using bikes to get from point A to point B or as a "dolly" to transport wood and food, while the kids play on bikes made from nothing but cut-and-tied tree branches. In cities like Amsterdam or Copenhagen, you won't believe the numbers of people riding instead of driving—even during cold and rainy winters.

TRICKS OF THE TRADE

USB-Rechargeable Lights: Always at the Ready

Here's a cool lighting option for those of you always working away on your laptops: rechargeable LED lights you plug into a USB port. They're bright, compact, and always charged if you spend bunches of time on your computer. Check 'em out.

Here in the states, though, we don't have quite the cycling tradition the rest of the world does. Cheap gasoline and a relatively high standard of living have made it easier for Americans to use cars, but climate change, pollution issues, rising gas prices, and concerns about inactivity and obesity are slowly changing that.

Bicycling is simple, clean, inexpensive—and fun!—transportation. It also improves our health, and the health of our cities and planet. By cycling, you're solving a lot of problems just by turning your legs. Let's look at why cycling makes sense and how you can become a safe and eco-conscious bike commuter.

BENEFIT #1: ECO-KARMA

Current research says most car trips taken in the United States are short-less than three miles. Still, 78 percent of people jump in the car to cover these short distances. A few of us already use the bike for our short errands, but if only 3 percent more of these trips were by bike or foot, we'd save 2.4 billion gallons of gasoline and spare the atmosphere 21 million tons of CO_2—every year.

Thinking in billions and millions is impressive, but also hard to visualize, so let's take a look at the local level. Cars are the largest source of air pollution in towns and cities. Look at traffic jams and smog where you live. Check out the potholes. Cars make a pretty big impact on the world around us.

Now consider your bike. It's silent, clean, and doesn't impact anybody but you—and only in a good way! You're healthier, and you have a few more bucks in your pocket because you're not spending money on gas (but more on those two important factors in a minute).

As roads and cities become more crowded, cycling offers a cleaner, and sometimes even faster, way to travel. There's certainly some pollution generated in the manufacturing of bicycles, but once bikes are made, they contribute no smog, don't need gas, and they don't clog roads or crowd parking garages. In countries like the Netherlands and China, millions of people get to work, do their shopping, go out with friends, and get a workout by bike. Try to imagine your town with clearer skies, healthier people, and quieter streets.

BENEFIT #2: YOUR BODY WILL THANK YOU

Cycling doesn't just mean less carbon in the atmosphere or pumping less oil from the earth. Riding just a few minutes a day will make your heart and lungs stronger, protect you from obesity and diabetes, and make you, believe it or not, more alert at school or at work.

Childhood obesity causes a lot of problems today. Younger generations today may be at risk of living shorter lives than their parents. Cycling keeps your weight down by burning calories, and the exercise also greatly diminishes your chances of developing diabetes. The Centers for Disease Control and Prevention say we need just twenty-two minutes of moderate exercise daily to improve our health.

BENEFIT #3: YOUR WALLET WILL THANK YOU

Often, part of being young is being broke. It just comes with the territory. Think of your bike as a low-to-no-cost way of staying connected with friends, getting to work, or pedaling to lunch in between classes. The bike also lets you save your car—if you have one—for road trips and longer journeys, when you really need it.

Consider that the Internal Revenue Service (IRS)—the dreaded tax collector for the federal government—lets a driver deduct 55.5 cents for every mile driven during a business trip. That's the IRS's estimate for how much it costs to run a car, in terms of wear-and-tear on tires, insurance and fuel costs, maintenance, and so on. So for every mile you pedal (or take the public bus or carpool) instead of drive, you're putting at least 55 cents in your pocket. Keep track of everywhere you go in the course of a week, then add it up. Imagine giving yourself that handful of cash.

BENEFIT #4: INDEPENDENCE

As a kid growing up, I rode all over south Denver, not just to mess around with my buddies, but also to get to the movies, soccer practice, school, and eventually to hang with my girlfriend. At any age, the bike is the cheapest way besides walking to get from point A to point B, and before you have your driver's license it's a way to get around without having to bug your parents.

BENEFIT #5: A MORE MOBILE LIFE

Another great benefit of bike commuting is that you can still carry lots of stuff with you: guitars, skis, groceries, costumes for Burning Man—you name it. There are panniers, messenger bags, built-in racks, and other packs designed to help carry anything you're strong enough to haul along on your ride.

ADVOCACY

If cycling as transportation seems like a good idea to you, then consider becoming an advocate for "active transportation." There are dozens of great organizations (keep reading for a few to get you started) doing everything from Rails to Trails projects, to winning federal funding for local transportation, to lobbying in Washington, DC for cycling-related issues.

Though politicians seem to get stuck at the national level, city and state officials have made surprising progress in transforming our transportation infrastructure to a more cycling-friendly one. Places like Portland, Oregon, and Davis, California, and even New York City, have constructed hundreds of miles of bike paths, included bikes in public transportation projects, and made their cities far more livable by incorporating bike facilities into the transportation mix.

Ask around or surf the internet a bit and see what organizations appeal to you. It's a worthwhile endeavor (and it also looks great on a college application).

Organizations That Can Help

Across the United States, there are dozens of organizations and thousands of people doing great work in the bike world. Check out these groups, or get involved in your community to help make the bike a bigger part of the future.

- The Sierra Club (SierraClub.org): Once just an "environmental" organization, the Sierra Club has expanded its vision to work on transportation and political issues. Keep in mind the club is "pro bike" in some situations (transportation) and "anti bike" in others (wilderness areas and habitat protection).
- Bikes Belong Coalition (BikesBelong.org): Bikes Belong advocates across the spectrum for cycling projects, as well as healthier lifestyles.
- People For Bikes (PeopleForBikes.org): People For Bikes advocates for a better future for cycling, tackling dozens of issues, so sign its online pledge and get involved.
- Rails to Trails Conservancy (RailstoTrails.org): These folks started by converting unused railroad corridors to cycling trails. Since 1986, they've helped build nineteen thousand miles of rail-trails, with another nine thousand miles slated for construction.
- BiketoWorkInfo.org: Simple, effective advice on leaving your car at home.
- BicyclingInfo.org: Great advice on dozens of topics.

- The League of American Bicyclists (BikeLeague.org): One of the oldest bike organizations in the United States, the League works on a variety of cycling issues.

- International Mountain Bicycling Association (imba.com): IMBA is the worldwideleader in mountain bike trail–building and advocacy. (often flashing) will help a lot. Reflective stickers on your bike make you a bit more visible, too. You can buy these at bike shops, hardware stores, or online.

Joe Breeze: A Founding Father of Mountain Biking Turned Bike Advocate

By Joe Breeze and Rob Coppolillo

I asked Joe five quick questions on saving the planet by bike, and he took the time to give us some great answers.

Rob: How do you see cycling becoming a larger part of our transportation lifestyles in the future?

Joe: Simple awareness of the power of bikes is key. The fact that you can propel yourself so easily around town aboard a bike equipped for the needs of daily transport was, until recently, practically a secret in this country. It's now one of those "Duh!" things. To everyone who tries it, it is a revelation. Riding where you need to go gets you into good shape, saves you money, helps the planet, and is fun. Cycling is the most efficient form of transit ever devised. Per calorie, you can travel three to four times quicker on a bike than by walking. You feel it as soon as you start to ride, and the effort you put into pedaling zips you along in a surprising way.

For local trips, chances are you can get there faster on a bike than with any other mode of travel. On the typical bike ride to school, for instance, you ride past long lines of cars slowed by other cars—while still obeying every traffic law. Not only do you not have to circle around for a parking place, you also did not have to work extra hours paying for a car, gas, and insurance. All expenditures considered, when a car is passing you, you are actually passing it.

The biggest reward is that your energy from riding gives you energy. It keeps you fit and healthy. In the morning, it wakes you up for the day; on the way, home it relieves stress.

Communities across America are figuring out that creating safer ways to bike offers the biggest bang for the buck in keeping America healthy.

Rob: What are the most important considerations when starting to commute by bike?

Joe: #1: Get equipped. I did a fair number of errands by bike when all I had was a "naked" bike, but until I had a fully equipped bike (with a kickstand, rack, full fenders, chainguard, and generator lights), I didn't know the extraordinary change it would have on my life.

#2: Get smart. Boost your confidence by taking a bike education program. Seek out experts in your area. Perhaps there's a bike coalition or similar group. Study and follow the motor-vehicle code as if your life depended on it. Ride like an ambassador of cycling.

#3: Get oriented. Study the best routes available. Local maps are a great resource. Maybe there are quieter side streets and shortcuts.

#4: Get dressed. I'm not talking Lycra, but everyday clothes that are versatile and make riding comfortable in a broad range of weather.

#5: Get going. The hardest part can be getting out the door with your bike. Once you do, the smile appears, and you'll wonder why it ever seemed so hard.

Rob: Are there any teen-specific issues related to bike commuting?

Joe: I asked my seventeen-year-old son, and he couldn't think of any negatives. He's ridden to school just about every day of his life. Beyond cycling's well-worn trail to freedom and adventure, a strong cycling community can create more opportunities. My son, Tommy, and his riding buddies have been the California State High School Mountain Bike Champions (NICA affiliate) for three years running. They're going for number four in 2012.

Rob: Your life has, in large part, been rooted in cycling. What's drawn you to the sport? What keeps you involved?

Joe: I raced at the highest level of road racing in this country, and I had the most wins of anyone in the first mountain bike race series, Repack. But really, what has fired me up all along in cycling is how intrinsic it can be to daily living. Cycling is much more than a sport. It's a lifelong blessing.

Rob: How did you end up becoming a transportation guru, from a background in mountain biking and racing?

Joe: In the 1950s, my father commuted by bike to his job as machinist and owner of the Sports Car Center in Sausalito (just across the Golden Gate Bridge from San Francisco). His interest was lightweight, efficient vehicles. I learned from him that bicycles are the king of efficiency. That was essentially the secret of cycling. My eyes were opened to the total breadth of cycling and I embraced it all. In the embryonic world of US cycling around 1970, I naturally became the go-to guy in my area. My pioneering role in mountain biking (in 1977 I built the first successful purpose-built mountain bikes) and a successful line of Breezer mountain bikes provided me a platform to expand on my lifelong interest in transportation cycling—and to become a pioneer in transportation bicycles for the United States.

Joe Breeze is probably best known for his pioneering role in mountain biking. A lifelong Marin County resident and bicycling advocate, he has bicycled California's highways and byways as a tourist, road racer, mountain biker, and commuter. A bicycle frame builder and designer since 1974, he was instrumental in the birth of the mountain bike with his "Breezer" bikes. He is a founding member of the National Off-Road Bicycling Association (NORBA), which is now part of USA Cycling. In 1998, he helped found the Marin County Bicycle Coalition, which focuses on bicycle transportation advocacy and works to improve infrastructure and cycling conditions. For more information, see www.breezerbikes.com.

9

PUTTING YOUR BIKE TO WORK

Eight chapters into this adventure, and with any luck, you're hooked. Whether it's BMX, entering your first race, or just riding your bike to school, cycling is fun in a hundred different ways. Now, here's a question for you: Have you considered making a little money at it? I'm not talking about trying your hand in the Tour de France, but how about getting paid to do what you love? It may sound too good to be true, but I'm bicycling proof that even a slacker can pay the bills by working in the bike world.

Think about how many different activities go into manufacturing cycling equipment, introducing people to the sport, maintaining the equipment, advertising related products, or advocating for bicycling as a transportation or lifestyle choice. I have a buddy who lobbies in Washington for cycling projects, another one who designs and markets high-end mountain bikes, and another who's a massage therapist traveling with a team.

The cycling industry offers you dozens of ways to make a living, and here are a few ideas to get you started.

BEFORE CASH, THERE'S CREDIT

No, not credit cards, but school credit. If you're in school, getting good grades is your job, so parlay your love of cycling into credit with your school. How? Start a cycling team. Intern at a local bike shop or in the office at a messenger company. Find work with a cycling-related non-profit in your community. In short, be creative, and then sell your school on the idea of some real-world study. Getting school credit doesn't have

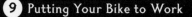

to mean a lot of boring work, and in fact, there's no rule against loving what you're doing, so go for it. And if you can finagle a little cash for the work, then so much the better.

Visit your guidance or career counselor at school and ask about self-directed or independent study. Get a clear idea about what you'd need from your employer or what kinds of documentation you'll need from your own venture and get moving. Be creative and try to include some interesting angles in your project. If you're creating a bike-to-school program, then highlight the environmental component. For example, how many fewer cars would be on the road? How many pounds of carbon emissions would it prevent?

With some hard work and a dash of freethinking, you should be able to snag yourself some credit—and have a little fun in the process. Better than calculus, right?

HIGHER EDUCATION ON TWO WHEELS

Suppose the powers-that-be at your school don't go for credit. No sweat. All is not lost, since it will still look great on your college application if you start your school's mountain bike racing team. Or you can start a nonprofit that provides refurbished bikes to disadvantaged kids in your town. Or implement that bike-to-school program. In other words, think big and don't be afraid to brag about yourself (politely and honestly, of course!) on your college resume and applications. You'll look impressive for doing something as relevant and as enviro as a cycling-related venture. Check in with your college counselor and perhaps she or he will have some helpful advice about how to explain your work in writing.

THE BIKE INDUSTRY: MORE FUN THAN WALL STREET

Sure, you'll make more money selling mutual funds or managing mergers than you will fixing bikes, but will you have more fun? Be more fulfilled? You'll need to answer that for yourself, but getting paid to do what you love is a rare gift, and it's one worth fighting for, even if it involves a few compromises.

In general, bike jobs pay a bit less than those in other industries, but that's partly because they offer a lifestyle and work environment with lots of perks. At the renowned cycling magazine *Velo*, many staffers— bosses and employees alike—take longer lunches to do group rides together. Companies like Chris King Precision Components, makers of the best headsets in the business, financially reward employees who ride their bikes to work. Sure, you might not make as much as your stock broker buddy or the one per centers of the world—but you'll probably have more fun and stay in better shape!

THE ALL-IMPORTANT "PRO DEAL"

Another major perk is the "pro deal." Once you're working in the industry, companies will begin letting you purchase certain items, including whole bikes, at handsome discounts—the hallowed pro deal. Companies offer pro deals (typically half the retail price) to people within the industry as a favor, but also because they like having "insiders" riding their stuff. If you get a job at a shop or intern at a magazine, you'll get instant insider status, and many companies will be psyched to have you showing off their gear. A 50 percent discount on all your cycling equipment—not bad, eh?

Job Hunting in the Bike World

The digital age keeps us connected and moving at a mile a minute. Check out these resources to get a jump on the competition in finding your cycling career. Jobs in the bike industry are highly sought after, both because they're fun, and also because many bike companies are in desirable locations like Northern and Southern California, and Portland, Oregon. If you're interested in snagging a position with a good, fun company, then start gaining experience now. Work in a shop, get an internship, and yeah—study hard!

BicycleIndustryJobs.com

OutdoorIndustryJobs.com

@JobsInCycling on Twitter

WORKING AT THE CORNER STORE

We keep talking about "your local bike shop," and hopefully you've found a great one by now. Well guess what? They need friendly, knowledgeable, no-attitude staff on the floor and at the mechanic stand, and you might be just the smiling face they're willing to pay to be there. Interested?

Even before you're up to speed in the world of cycling, you might be able to help keep your favorite shop swept up and looking neat. Intern for a month. Tell them you're interested in learning the ropes, with the specific goal of working there. You won't get rich, but down the road you could manage the place, or eventually meet people at different bike brands and work for them. You'll learn a ton working at a bike shop, and it's a great foot-in-the-door to the bike world.

MESSENGERS

Spend ten minutes on the corner in any big city, and you're bound to see a brave man or woman tear by on a fixie. Chances are they'll have a tattered messenger bag slung across their back and be gone before you can say "no gears and no brakes."

Messengers are the unsung environmental heroes of the urban landscape. They don't look like traditional tree huggers, but they save millions of miles of driving every year, cut down on traffic congestion, and improve our air quality. They also have a blast riding around town.

If you're lucky enough to work in a city with a messenger company, ask them if they need anybody to help out in the office or run packages. You don't necessarily need a fixie for messenger work, though most couriers these days ride them. You will definitely need a helmet and a bombproof lock, though; messengers fall occasionally, and anywhere there are bikes, there are thieves. Watch out!

SOMEBODY HAS TO MAKE THE NEXT COOL BIKE

Any successful bike brand has a cast of engineers and designers making their products lighter, faster, stronger, and sexier. If you like tinkering and aesthetics, then maybe this part of the bike biz is for you. The best custom bike builders on the planet now work in the United States, rather than Italy or France, so there are plenty of places to learn hands-on skills—welding, brazing, carbon lay-up—as well as bike design. Visit the North American Handmade Bicycle Show (NAHBS), and you'll meet dozens of artisans, any one of whom could be your future boss.

If design is your path, then start taking engineering and art classes. There are good programs across the country, including prestigious ones like the Rhode Island School of Design (RISD). You'll need good grades for programs like California College of the Arts and RISD, so study hard and meet some folks in the bike industry. Designing bikes would be a pretty cool gig out of college. Put your mind to it and make it happen.

Parlez-vous "Bike Guide," Monsieur?

Why not get paid to tour around Europe on your bike? I fell into this opportunity when I met my good buddy Andy Hampsten. Hampsten won the 1988 Tour of Italy and finished fourth at the Tour de France on two occasions. The racing was all well and good, but his real lifetime achievement is starting a bike-touring company based in Italy. Pure genius!

Get this—he actually pays me to ride around with guests, showing them the sights, eating the best food, and drinking the best wine on the planet, and occasionally lifting a suitcase or two. World's greatest job. Period.

Now, before you quit school and book a flight to Pisa, there are a few skills you'll need to get hired. You'll help set yourself ahead of the crowd by a) learning the language of the country in which you'd like to work, b) learning how to perform basic bike repairs, and c) getting to know said country's history and cuisine. If you're into Spain, then study up. France? No problem; people love riding in France. Italy? No brainer. Just learn as much as you can, get conversational in the language, and start applying with tour groups. Offer to intern first, but once they get a load of your epic skills, you'll be hired in no time. Side benefit: If you travel in a foreign country, you're bound to meet other contacts, and the dream in a cool city like Lyon, France, or Girona, Spain. Good luck!

SOIGNEURS AND PRO WRENCHES

Professional cycling teams employ "soigneurs"—the people who take care of the riders—and mechanics (often called "wrenches"). Soigneur means "caretaker" or "trainer" in French, and generally these folks are massage therapists, but you could also be a physical therapist, chiropractor, or Rolfer. Mechanics are often ex-riders or shop veterans who can fix bikes on the fly and survive life on the road.

Soigneurs feed the riders during the races and give them massages after the finishes. Wholesome food and therapeutic massage helps the athletes' recovery and prevents injuries. Soigneurs can also be in charge of logistics and may manage gear between races, but that depends on the team and how many other staffers they have. Soigneurs work long hours, but they get to travel a bunch, and they have a blast between events.

Mechanics get the same travel perks as soigneurs, and, like soigneurs, they work long hours into the night, repairing bikes or preparing them for the following day's race. By the end of a cycling season, all the mechanics seem to be buddies, forming a kind of traveling circus. It's tough work, but you'll meet people from Europe, Australia, New Zealand, and all over the United States.

Sure, you'll work yourself to the bone, but having met a slew of these folks, I can say they are cool, cultured, and fun to party with. Sound like your thing? Work in a shop and learn the craft, or get through massage school, then introduce yourself to the teams.

THE GLAMOROUS LIFE OF A WRITER

I got lucky and fell into cycling journalism at the age of twenty. Boulder, where I was going to college, was home to two cycling-related magazines, so it was easy for me to slip a few articles past the editors before they

TRICKS OF THE TRADE

Open Doors—With a Press Pass

If you end up pursuing journalism, one of the perks is getting an international or national press accreditation. There are a few different organizations that issue them. Having a press card opens lots of doors, and it also scores you discounts at museums and cultural events. Plus, you feel pretty cool busting out the press card. Get a few articles published and then look into the National Writers Union for starters.

realized how young I was. Fortunately, in the journalism world an editor cares more about getting a good, well-researched story on time than college degrees and credentials.

Writing can be a flexible, fun, entertaining career, but it's not for everybody. The money comes and goes, depending on how many stories/articles you sell in a month. At the time, this didn't stress me out, though some of my friends thought I was nuts. If you're pretty laid back in terms of finances and can string a few words together, then maybe you should consider the pen.

Writing is a blast because you can literally do it anywhere. Interested in Mexico's version of the Tour de France, the Ruta Mexico? Find a newspaper or magazine willing to cover an off-the-beaten-path race, and sell them on the idea. Maybe you're an environmentalist and you want people to hear about the really cool Rails-to-Trails program. Organizations like Rails-to-Trails need writers to pen their newsletters and press releases, so try an internship, and if you're lucky you might slide into a job. Every bike catalog you see was written by somebody. Get to know a company's products and that somebody could be you.

Writing is just a skill like bricklaying or being an electrician. Companies need people to communicate their messages constantly, so if you can write, get yourself in the door and show them what you can do. The bike world has plenty of races, brands, and personalities, so pay attention in English class and keep your eyes peeled for stories to tell, and then tell them!

DOING GOOD

There's so much inherent good in cycling, it's no wonder there are dozens of nonprofits spreading the gospel of our two-wheeled church. Nationally and internationally there are groups like Bikes Belong and World Bicycle Relief (WorldBicycleRelief.org) working hard to improve people's lives and communities with the bike.

All of these organizations need motivated, hard-working people to administer their programs, fundraise, and educate the public. Again, you won't get rich quick pursuing nonprofit work, but you can help effect positive change and make a living in the sport you love.

MAKING THE BIKE YOUR BUSINESS

Hopefully you're a bit closer to making a living doing what you love—riding! Believe in yourself, pay attention to the opportunities, and you're likely to find a bicycling salary out there somewhere. When you make your millions, drop me a line, and let me know how it feels to be rich and powerful.

July 2000—The Ultimate Assignment

By Rob Coppolillo

I saw the lights of a gas station ahead, and knew it was my last chance: electricity. The battery on my laptop had died, and I needed to plug in—desperately, too, because I had a deadline, and it was nearly midnight.

The 2000 Tour de France would end a week later, with Lance Armstrong winning for the second time in two years. I was writing for a website in Austin, Texas, and I owed them an article by the end of their business day, which was right about now! Problem was, it was the middle of the night, outside Briançon, France, and I was outta juice.

Into the gas station I went, armed with my smile, decent Italian, and broken French. With armaments like these, I stood a 20 percent chance of getting anything done.

"Bonsoir," I began.

Ten minutes later, after much gesturing and saying "oui, oui" I was in business, sitting on the floor, typing furiously. The manager made it clear: I had ten minutes to send my story.

These were the days before wireless, mind you. I had a modem card, which felt ubercool and totally modern at the time. I typed and downloaded pics, then zipped them into a file, then emailed them via my clunky laptop's cellular connection. It was phoning in a story, just like newspapermen had done seventy-five years before, but honestly, sitting there in a Total gas station in shorts and sandals, speaking French and Italian with the proprietor, covering one of the world's largest sports events—I felt cool.

Exhausted, harried, stressed, sure, but man, it was a blast. I had the company credit card, I'd already been in France for two weeks, and I'd party in Paris in a matter of days with riders and journalists from around the world. And this was work.

I've made a tiny bit of money racing, quite a bit of cash writing about racing, and enough dough to cover the wine bills guiding bike trips, so I say I've had a good career in cycling so far. This book is just the latest chapter in my two-wheeled journey.

Yes, I've branched out beyond the bike, but it will always be part of my life. Now that my wife and I have two sons, it's like starting over in a way. They're already pushing a little four-wheeled scooter around the living room, and pretty soon they'll be racing down the sidewalk on balance bikes, squawking at me to keep up. The bike's a cool way to live your life, and if you can make a little spending money with it, so much the better.

The Tour de France in 2000 will be a tough assignment to beat, but there's always hope. Helicopter skiing, diving with sharks, the professional donut critic—you never know, maybe some other epic assignment will come along. For now, though, that July was the real deal.

10

PINNING ON
A NUMBER

With only a few exceptions (I'm talking to you, LeMond and Lance), biking won't make you famous or rich, and what you see at the Tour de France is hard, painful, and dangerous—but if racing is your thing, it can be incredibly fun and totally worth it. By now you've found a bike and gotten it dialed, so let's figure out what kind of race you're going to enter and get you to the finish line! It's time to make the jump to pinning on a number and throwing down.

Competitive cyclists form a tight group, and if you choose to join it, you'll make great friends that will follow you through life. The long hours of training, the travel to events, and the fulfillment of meeting your goals—and watching your friends meet theirs—create lasting friendships. My nephew is now thirteen, and he's doing 'cross races with his best friend. They race together, train together, and goof off plenty. He's on the way to a bunch of fun as a teenager. Pretty cool to watch.

FINDING A RACE

Many states, like Colorado, Texas, and Tennessee, have their own organizations devoted specifically to competitive cycling—be it road, mountain, cyclo-cross, or BMX. If your state doesn't have its own competitive cycling organization, there's also USA Cycling, the national governing body for the sport, which helps organize and promote competitive cycling, so a little internet searching will put you on the right track without much hassle. Search for the name of your hometown or state, "bike races," and "calendar," and you'll be in business.

Make sure not to cut things too close. Instead, look for a race a few weeks or months down the road. This will give you plenty of time to get prepped and figure out the ins and outs of your chosen event. And speaking of your event, choose one that seems fun for more than just the cycling: Perhaps it's in a town or park you've always wanted to visit, or maybe it's a hilly road race that appeals to the climber in you, or if speed's your thing maybe it's a flat-and-fast cyclo-cross course. And by the same token, avoid races you won't enjoy.

IT'S PREP TIME

Once you're set on an event, it's time to get ready. Competitive cyclists spend years, even decades, gradually improving and training. The fitness gains work on two levels: short-term and long-term. You'll be able to make some good progress over the course of just a few months, but year to year you'll be amazed, if you stick with it, at how much stronger you'll become. Don't stress about piling on the training miles and trying to win the world championships your first year. If you recognize it's your first season and create your goals accordingly, you'll set yourself up to have a ton of fun and meet a bunch of cool, like-minded friends.

Rather than counting on winning ten grand at your first race, focus on finishing the entire event and riding just as well at the end as you do at the start. You'll be amazed at how fast some of the competition is; chances are they've been doing it for years already. Luckily for you, though, lots of events offer different categories for more- and less-experienced riders. Set your sights on finishing the race and learning the ropes—and leave the hard-core competition for another race or two.

SAFETY FIRST

Safety is important. Seriously. It might not be first on your list of weekend priorities, but bike racing—whether it's BMX, cyclo-cross, track, road, or mountain—means going as fast as you can with a bunch of other people going as fast as they can alongside you. And when you get that many people bombing through corners, hopping over logs, and sprinting for the win, things can get dicey in a hurry. Get yourself ready by practicing with some friends. Even if they're not interested in racing, just ask them to humor you a bit.

The Hairless Option

To shave or not to shave, that is the question. Nearly all competitive road cyclists do it and many mountain bikers, too. It's not for aerodynamics, as many people think, but rather for facilitating massage and staying clean in the event of a crash. Massage therapists will tell you it's far nicer to rub a shaved leg than a hairy one (imagine rubbing lotion onto your dog— gross!) and should you ever crash your bike—and if you race, you eventually will—your wounds will stay cleaner without hair on them. Do you need to shave? If you choose not to, it won't slow you down, but shaving does get you in the mindset of a serious rider. Your non-cycling friends might heckle you if you're a guy, but your cycling friends will expect it. Your call!

First off, find a grassy field, hop on your bikes, and practice staying upright in a crowd by riding in a group and bumping into one another— gently at first, then with more force. Be reasonable—you're not trying to knock anybody over. You're just getting used to the sensation of being bumped while riding. This will prepare you for the inevitable chaos of a race, where riders zig and zag and occasionally collide. You may want to wear plain tennis shoes for your practice sessions, so you're not clipped in and you can easily put down a foot to prevent yourself from crashing. Start slowly, then increase your tempo a bit, and finally let your buddies bump you hard enough to make you swerve. Keep your upper body loose and relaxed and absorb the shock of them hitting you, rather than tensing up and being sent flying. With just a bit of practice, you'll be impossible to knock off!

As you become more comfortable on your bike, practice cornering at higher speeds. Always wear cycling gloves while training and racing because you'll want to protect your hands if you fall. Find a safe, quiet parking lot if you're preparing for a road race or "criterium"—a shorter, faster event with more corners. An abandoned field or lot will work for a 'cross or mountain bike race. If you're lucky enough to live near a velodrome or BMX track, see if they offer free time for juniors, or better yet, an orientation class. In short, think ahead to your event and try to duplicate some of the challenges you'll face, that way it won't be totally foreign to you when the starting gun goes—BANG!

Bike racing techniques and tactics become more complicated the further down the rabbit hole you go. For example, you'll gradually learn that, in a road race, there are lots of ways to save energy, like sitting in the draft of the rider ahead of you. If you're interested in learning more, check your local library or look online for books on cycling tactics and bike racing. No matter what discipline it is, somebody has written an interesting, informative book on how to do it better.

And when you finally go to your first race, keep in mind that the most important thing is having fun. Don't feel like you've got to go faster than you've ever gone before. You'll get there eventually, but when you're starting out, don't pressure yourself or take unnecessary risks. You have hundreds of bike races in your future if you want them, so ease into it and enjoy the ride.

NOBODY WINS BIKE RACES NAKED (EXCEPT AT BURNING MAN)

Let's talk clothing. Don't worry about having the latest, greatest cycling jersey and shorts. Everyone's first race is a learning experience, and it's usually pretty overwhelming, so if you can piece together an inexpensive outfit—or "kit," as pros call their shoes, shorts, jerseys, hats, and gloves—then you're in good shape. (See Chapter 3 for help finding online bargains.) If you'd rather save your hard-earned cash, then just find a decent pair of cycling shorts, wear a close-fitting T-shirt, and you're good to go.

The next most important piece of gear (besides a helmet, because you're already wearing a helmet every ride, right?!) is a pair shoes. You certainly don't need to have cycling shoes to compete, but eventually, even if you're just riding for fun, you'll want cycling shoes with cleats on them. You can spend $500 on handmade Italian shoes crafted of kangaroo leather—no joke—but even most top amateurs don't go that deep. Keep your eyes peeled for a bargain, online or at your local shop you should be able to pick up a pair for less than $100.

KEEPING COOL ON RACE DAY

Reducing stress is the name of the game come race day, so do your homework the night before. Make sure you know where you're going (not only where the race is, but where to park) and what the weather forecast is so you can bring appropriate clothing. Get a good night's rest and don't eat anything too heavy within three hours of your race. You don't want to hurl in your first event. A light snack is OK (like an energy bar or piece of fruit), but go for steak and eggs and you'll volcano-puke for sure.

TRICKS OF THE TRADE

Pinning on a Number

You might be thinking, what's the big deal? You get your race number and pin it on, right? Wrong! First off, crumple up your number and then smooth it out. Then take your safety pins and, instead of pinning your number right at the corners (with one side of the pin on the jersey and the other on the number), pin it about two centimeters away from the edge (toward the center of the number) at each corner and once in the middle.

Now the pins are on top of the number, holding it against your body. Because you crumpled it, the edges are irregular and won't catch air like a parachute, which would slow you down and be annoying. See that? You just got faster and the race hasn't even begun. Cut me in for some of your race winnings, OK?

If you don't have a buddy to pin you, then take off your jersey and do it on your lap. Push the safety pin down through the number and jersey, and then come up through the jersey and through the number. (Practice at home with a piece of paper if this sounds confusing.)

Arrive at your race two hours in advance. This will leave you plenty of time to register, get your number, and locate the start and finish lines, as well as mechanical support, should it be available. Once you're there, get your number and pay your entry fee. If you're registering as a "junior," or an under-eighteen competitor, keep in mind that many races divide juniors into different age groups (10–12, 13–14, and so on). If you're lucky, your race will be free—but don't count on it. Make sure you've got cash or a check from your parents. You'll also need Mom, Dad, or a guardian to sign your entry form. When you're paid up, the registration folks will give you your number. Double-check your start time with them, too.

Senior Citizens

If you're nineteen or older, then you'll race with the "seniors." This always sounded weird to me, being a "senior" at the age of twenty-four, but hey, that's what the governing body calls riders over nineteen. Occasionally you'll see under-twenty-three races, but usually only at larger events.

If you're nineteen or older, no sweat. You'll have to sign the same forms as the juniors, but you'll be able to sign for yourself. You'll be racing against riders much older (in some cases in their forties), but you'll register in the easiest category and just start working your way up. Most of the older riders will be cool, so get in there, watch what the good guys do, and go for it.

After you've pinned on your number and gotten dressed, it's time to warm up. You'll want at least a half-hour of easy riding, so find some safe roads nearby. Bring along a windtrainer (a device that lets you pedal in place, without moving) if you'd rather get a warm-up near the starting line. If you're racing cyclo-cross, BMX, or a mountain bike, then try to preride the course—but only if the course marshals allow it. You don't want to get in trouble with the race officials before the gun goes off.

After you're warm and loose (after at least ten minutes of spinning), do a few fifteen-second sprints to really open up. This is like getting the engine of your car ready to go at top speed. Three or four of these and you'll be ready to rock.

GETTING TO THE FINISH LINE

Get to the starting line with ten or fifteen minutes to spare. Riders begin lining up several minutes before the start, so if you show up thirty seconds before the referee blows the whistle, you'll be stuck in the back of the bunch. If you're early, you get "staged" in the front, which is like getting a head start on the riders in the back. You'll also be able to get up to speed without anyone falling over in front you or slowing you down, which, believe me, happens all the time. Not to me, though. Never. Not even once. OK, maybe once. Or twice.

Relaxed Racing—Benefit Rides and "Gran Fondos"

If the speed and chaos of racing sounds a little much, then consider doing a benefit ride or gran *fondo*. There are plenty of benefit or charity rides to choose from—from multi-day tours down the California coast to one-day centuries (one-hundred-mile rides) to twenty-mile jaunts—in just about every part of the country. Some are fully supported with food and rest stops, while others are more "do-it-yourself," so look for one that benefits a cause that's dear to you and sign up. You get all the fun and experience of riding with a big bunch, but none of the stress and pressure of a race.

Loosely translated, gran *fondo* is Italian for a "big ride," but there are also gran *fondi* for running races and ski events, too. These are split-personality events because the folks at the front are racing, while the rest of us are just focused on making it to the finish. They're fun, generally faster than a benefit ride, and often hosted by professional cyclists like Tour of California champ Levi Leipheimer.

Benefit ride or gran *fondo*—they're fun, a great way to meet people, and a good opportunity to ride some new roads.

In a road, 'cross, or mountain-bike race, the officials will make you start with one foot on the ground, so make sure you've practiced by taking a couple of pedal strokes and then clipping in and getting going. BMX starts are a little trickier, as you'll be in a start gate and maybe on a little hill, with both feet on the pedals. Whatever your event, practice your starts so you're able to stay at the front for the first thirty seconds of the race.

Once the gun goes off and you're moving, settle in to your own pace and keep it there. Don't get suckered into breaking a speed record, because after five or ten minutes, you'll get tired and fall back. Ride at your own pace, and pay attention to the course and riders ahead of you.

Usually there's a timing clock or set of cards that lets you know how much time or how many laps remain in the race. If it's a road race, you'll know how many miles the course is, and if you have a cycling computer you can watch it to gauge your efforts. Remember, you'll pay for starting out too hard, so if anything, go a little easier than you think you need to in the beginning, and conserve energy for the second half of the race.

Before you know it, the finish line will be in sight. If you're riding with other riders, chances are they'll sprint to try and move up a couple of places in the finishing order. This is one of the most exciting parts of the sport! Go as fast as you can, but keep your head up so you can see if somebody swerves toward you or if there's a slower rider ahead.

STAYING FIT

So you did your first race—congrats! Well, did you like it? I trust you survived with all your limbs intact and you got a good night's rest after the race. Ready for another one, maybe in a week or a month, or two?

Chances are you'll want to improve a bit, so start riding more and getting comfortable with the speed and physical demands. Bike racing asks a lot of your bod, so you'll need to be focused on your diet, staying hydrated, and sleeping well (seven to nine hours hours a night) consistently—not just the night before your races.

Competition develops great habits that will follow you through life. If you're paying attention, it teaches you a bunch about your body, mind, and self. To get the most out of your racing, you'll need to eat wholesome, clean food. You can still indulge once in a while (or a few times a week if you're a weakling like me!), but in general, you need lean proteins like salmon and chicken, healthy fats like olive oil, and complex carbohydrates like brown rice and whole-grain breads. Combine those with some training, be in bed by 10 pm, and you're good to go

TURNING PRO

If you catch the bug big-time, then it's time to get serious. Try as many different races as you can, both in terms of terrain (hills, flats, tricky courses) and disciplines (road, mountain, track, BMX). Figure out what you like and go with it. You'll meet cool people, and you can start traveling to races with them; sooner or later, you'll find a team to join. Train and race with fun, supportive friends and you will love the camaraderie. (I don't miss the racing all that much, but I sure miss the long days training with friends, laughing it up, and having adventures along the road.)

Watch the best riders at the races or on training rides, and learn from them. How do they dress in the cold? What do they eat and drink during the race? How much do they cool down after the finish line? Don't hesitate to approach professionals and ask them about training, equipment, and tactics. Most pros are super friendly and love helping out younger riders. Take advantage of it. If there's a big pro race nearby, get to it—you won't believe how fast they're going: Uphill, downhill, in the corners—they're amazing athletes.

WHAT TO WATCH TO GET INSPIRED

There are a few classic cycling films and races that every cyclist should watch. These definitely helped me on days when I was lacking motivation for an event or indoor training session. I'd pop in a DVD (actually, back in the day, it was a VHS tape) and get psyched. Check these out for starters:

- *American Flyers*, one of Kevin Costner's break-out roles, about two brothers making it in professional road racing
- *The 1989 Tour de France,* Greg LeMond's miraculous eight-second victory
- *The 1989 World Championships,* LeMond's spectacular win over Irishman Sean Kell
- *Kranked*—revolutionary, mind-blowing footage of mountain biking in Vancouver and beyond. Unbelievable riding and a great soundtrack—pure entertainment
- *Seasons,* follows professional freeriders, downhillers, and racers through four seasons, giving you a glimpse of what it's like to live the life
- Anything by "The New World Disorder," these guys emphasize going huge on the mountain bike.
- And for street/trials, two words, friends: Danny MacAskill. Visit his site, www.DannyMacAskill.co.uk and click on "Videos." And then, hang on

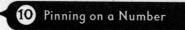

The Joy of Junior Racing

By Andy Hampsten

I thought I was too late entering the bike racing game when I started at fifteen. The fastest kids were driven to races by their parents, to hot beds of racing culture like Ames, Iowa, and Milwaukee, Wisconsin. Me? I would ride eighty miles to Fargo, just to catch a ride in the back of a pickup overnight to races in South Dakota.

But I had the advantages of obscurity and racing ignorance in my corner. When I was sixteen, I hitched two rides to get myself to Madison, Wisconsin, where I had made friends the summer before with a kid named Mike Cofrin. I showed up at Cofrin's house with my bike and duffel bag in tow. Mike answered the door and was a bit surprised to see me, but remembered we had talked about me coming for the summer.

"Just wait here while I ask my dad about it. I kinda forgot to tell him," he said.

I knew then and there I wanted to race bikes, race hard, and maybe win—and have the means to get a hotel when I needed one.

It actually worked out better than that. At sixteen, I was realizing that I needed to go easy on a world that didn't yet realize my genius. I'd use racing as a way to travel, hang out with fun people, hammer my body until it felt like parts would come out, and then see if anyone in my growing circle of friends wanted me sleeping on their floor at the next race, wherever that was. Washing dishes after a dinner or mowing a lawn at a host's house seemed like a great deal to be able to race around the country.

I worked in bike shops when I could and trained in the afternoons when my friends got out of school. Sometimes the wages made a lot more sense than racing for money, but I was still trying to make up time to beat the kids who started racing before me.

When I was seventeen, I needed to impress the national team coaches in the hopes of making the junior world championships team. I decided to race with the adults at the Memorial Day weekend races. Sunday was a slightly hilly course in Muscatine, Iowa. I made the front group with three other guys—all good, fast racers. I thought of just hanging on the back of them and not taking my turns at the front, but that would only get me shelled (left behind). I decided to ride hard at the front, but not foolishly so. My junior friends were going berserk, cheering for me to "just hang in there!" for dozens of laps.

In the final laps, two of the guys in the break told me that I'd better not contest the sprint because I "took an illegal feed." (I dropped my bottle with fruit juice, and picked it up off the curb on the next lap where my friends placed it.) I was getting weak in the break and was crazy excited to just finish with these guys if I could. Mike Farrell, who won most of the races, told the other guys: "Quit your moaning; the kid is riding great."

I sprinted to second behind Farrell, and felt like I'd won my own Tour de France.

Andy Hampsten is the only American man to have won the Tour of Italy, back in 1988. He also finished fourth in the Tour de France twice—in 1986, when he won the Best Young Rider award, and in 1992; that year, he won the infamous Alpe d'Huez stage of the three-week race. Born in North Dakota, he was far from the cycling scene of the 1960s and '70s, but he found his way into the sport, becoming one of the great riders of the '80s and early '90s. These days he guides bike tours in Italy with his wife, Elaine, and kids, Emma and Oscar.

11

ADVENTURE CYCLING

Adventure cycling ranges from year-long, 'round-the-world jour-neys to single-night stays in hotels just a few miles from home. You get to decide just how deep down the rabbit hole you want to ride. The bike opens doors you might otherwise roll right by. You'll meet friends, discover things about yourself, laugh lots, suffer some, and if you're inspired to hit the open road, you'll see places, people, and land-scapes wilder than you can believe. Touring—or adventure cycling—is your on-ramp to some amazing new experiences.

A few words of caution: For any bike trip longer than a few hours—and certainly any time you're spending a two-wheeled night away from home—planning is critical. Thorough planning will make you more comfortable, reduce your stress, and greatly increase your chances of returning with a happy story (instead of a horror story).

Adventure cycling also requires sharp route-finding skills and sound judgment, so you might want to have someone more experienced come along for your first few outings. Eventually you'll be ready for a trip with just your friends, or even a solo mission, but don't bite off more than you can chew just yet.

If you sleep in a nice warm bed every night, why hit the open road with your bike, sleeping in campgrounds or cheap motels? Answer: It's fun! It's a little bit intimidating, totally interesting, and usually exciting when you open the map, plot a course, and start pedaling, knowing you won't be coming home until—tomorrow, next week, or next year.

You'll be amazed, too, at how people approach you when you're on your bike. In a car with out-of-state plates, you might be looked at suspiciously or ignored altogether. On a bike, locals will walk right up to you and start chatting. Talk to veterans of the adventure cycling circuit, and they'll tell you stories of being offered hot meals and places to stay, and many keep in touch with folks they've met along their routes.

Sure, some people don't find the idea of adventure cycling any more appealing than backpacking or doing the hostel circuit in Europe, but if you do, now's the time to start exploring the big, wide world out there.

THE RIGHT BIKE FOR THE JOURNEY

You can tour on just about any kind of bike, but usually a road or mountain bike is the best call. Adventure cycling requires lower (easier) gears than you'll be used to, but keep in mind you might have an additional five, ten, or thirty pounds of stuff with you, so the hills will seem even tougher than usual. Traditional mountain bike gearing works well, but easier rear cogs on a road or cyclo-cross bike will keep you moving when you're laden with extra tonnage.

A dedicated touring bike is a luxury, and if you really get the bug you might want to think about one down the road. For now, though, any comfortable bike with twenty-six-inch or 700c wheels (typical mountain and road wheels, respectively) will probably work.

HAVE CREDIT CARD, WILL TRAVEL

The simplest form of adventure cycling is "credit-card touring." You decide on a location, plot a safe and scenic route to it, bring along the bare minimum in terms of gear, pack your (or your parents') credit card, and start pedaling. Having a card along means you can stop for food at restaurants, supermarkets, and convenience stores, and once you arrive at your destination, you can check into a hotel for the night.

If you've never used a card before, double-check with your parents and the company issuing the card that you can charge with it while away. Your folks can call their card's customer service department and let them know you'll be using it, so if a hotel or restaurant gives you problems, have them call the card company, which can then authorize the charge. Bring your ID, be polite, and you shouldn't have too much difficulty.

The Hardest Race of All

The Race Across America, or RAAM as cyclists know it, is about as simple as it gets: See who can race from the West Coast of the continental US to the East. Sure, there's a pre-scribed course, but beyond that, riders can sleep as little or as much as they want, stop for food or massages however often they see fit—whatever it takes to get to the finish.

Pete Penseyres set the record in 1986, crossing from Los Angeles to Atlantic City in eight days, nine hours, and forty-seven minutes. He slept as little as ninety minutes a night and derived 80 percent of his calories from liquid protein shakes. Riders typically enlist a large support staff, helping to feed them and drive alongside in a "SAG wagon" (see below) with spare clothing, extra wheels, and plenty of food!

Part race and part epic tour, RAAM is one of the world's hardest athletic endeavors.

YOUR GUARDIAN ANGEL: THE SAG WAGON

If you're looking for a little more support along the way, and perhaps a bit more adventure, then consider the SAG wagon, otherwise known as any sort of car, van, or truck that can follow along and carry your stuff. Depending upon whom you ask, SAG either stands for "Support and Gear," or it just refers to the way the vehicle "sags" behind you and your cycling buddies as you tick off the miles. Its meaning becomes less important when you seek refuge from the the searing heat or thunder-storms, feast on fresh fruit and chocolate bars, or change into clean cycling clothing, going from fatigued to psyched in two minutes flat.

The SAG wagon follows your tour, carrying spare gear, rain jackets, water, food, and camping gear, if you're planning on sleeping out. This liberates you from stopping in "civilized" spots for food and rest. Sometimes a group of cyclists takes turns with the driving/support duties: One rider will drive for the morning, while her buddies ride, and then she swaps out for the afternoon leg and another rider drives until dark. There are also organized tours on which the company provides SAG wagons for a few or a few dozen cyclists. It's a great way to tour, with a built-in safety net.

An SUV or minivan works great as a SAG vehicle. If you go with an organized tour, they'll have food, maps, and equipment all ready for you. Hit the web and check the end of this chapter for leads on finding a touring company if you go that route. If you're throwing together your own journey, you'll need to arrange your own food, maps, and camping equipment.

Get to Know: The ACA

A bike-crazed posse in Missoula, Montana, runs The Adventure Cycling Association (AdventureCycling.org), and I think they're on to something. Since 1973, they've helped people get on their bikes, pack light, plan well, and go big. When you think about it, planning your own bike trip is more being adventurous than being a tourist, so I use their term, adventure cycling, instead of bike touring. Makes more sense to me. Visit their site if you need help with maps, equipment, random questions, or just about any issue related to leaving home with your bike. If they don't have the answer, they'll connect you with someone who does.

Their "Pedal Pioneers" page is set up to help parents plan for cycling with kids, but give it a read as it will give you a few ideas, too.

STEPPING OUT ON YOUR OWN

After a few supported or organized tours, you might be ready to go it alone or in a small group. This requires meticulous planning so you don't end up at the campground at night with everyone wondering why no one brought the stove and what happened to the tent. Fully independent adventure cycling is the most committing style, and it's not for everybody.

THE ALL-IMPORTANT GEAR LIST

If a more independent tour sounds fun, you'll need a system for carry-ing your gear. This comes down to panniers or a trailer. Remember that panniers are essentially saddlebags for your bike, while a trailer rolls along behind you with all your gear tucked inside a waterproof cover. Both systems have their benefits and cyclists have gone around the world using each. Keep in mind that panniers require racks and a way to fasten them to your bike. A good shop can help you set this up, but it's another consideration to keep in mind.

With any tour, but self-supported ones in particular, your gear list is critical to staying comfortable and safe. You'll need to carefully plan:

- Your sleep system, including a tent
- Your food and drink, which is to say lots of both—and make it nutritious, too
- Spare parts for repairs
- Special parts like fatter tires for dirt roads and a smoother ride
- Your clothing, including rain gear or a sun hat for under your helmet
- Maps with your route, places to refuel, bike shops, and camp-grounds marked
- Your safety equipment, like front and rear lights and an orange visibility flag
- Cash, credit cards, a cell phone, and something to read at night

This is just for starters. Your gear list will have to take into account the weather you might experience, the time of year and probable tempera-tures, and the kind of riding you'll do—rough roads, big climbs, and possible hazards. Connecting with other cyclists online can help you fine-tune your list, as will some reading on AdventureCycling.org. Do your research, and your trip will run that much more smoothly.

SHIPPING YOUR BIKE

Traveling by train, air, or bus with a bike can be a hassle, no doubt. Bikes can break down and bikes and gear can get stolen, but it's generally worth the risk for the right trip. Let's review options. Numerous companies and services will ship your bike. Some adventurers mail their bike to and from their touring location. It's expensive, but it does save you some hassle and travel planning.

If you pack it yourself, you can ship via UPS or FedEx, or with a service like BikeFlights or Sports Express. Using these services to ship within the US is not unreasonably pricey, but as soon as you start shipping to Europe or beyond, expect to pay hundreds. Make sure your bike is insured on your parents' homeowners policy or with your renters insurance if you're living on your own. Some travel insurance policies will cover your ride, too—double-check the fine print because they sometimes have an exclusion for expensive computers, bikes, cameras, and the like.

Pedal Your Way to School Credit

Have you considered the possibility of getting some school credit for your efforts in cycling? Here's a great opportunity to do it: Organize a senior cycling trip, with an educational or service-oriented theme. How about riding a bunch of bikes up to the Sioux reservation in South Dakota? You can donate your bikes to interested teens on the res when you leave for home. You could also ride to other schools, talking about the environmental benefits of cycling as transportation. Find a friend who's interested in the project and dream something up.

Drop by Sprockids.com—it features a ton of information to get you rolling toward school credit and beyond.

BOXES

Any time you slap a mailing label on your bike, you're going to have to pack it, which means disassembling it and organizing it within a box or case. You can buy a plastic case for $199, and it'll do a great job of protecting your bike. Several manufacturers have models that are easy to use and really durable. These are great for shipping, and can also be checked as luggage on flights. Rates for flying with a bike vary; check before you book a ticket because some airlines charge as much as $200 each way, while others are free. What looks like a cheap ticket might be quite a bit more, once you pay a bike fee.

If your shop will help or if you're pretty crafty, you can fashion your own box. See if your shop has a cardboard box in which a new bike has just arrived. You can fit your disassembled bike into it, using cut sheets of cardboard to reinforce areas around the derailleurs. This takes a little trial and error, so see if an experienced mechanic will help. Bring him or her some treats for the effort (you can never go wrong with cookies—the universal currency).

For help on disassembling (and reassembling!) your bike, check online for video tutorials or pay your favorite mechanic a few bucks to show you how the first time. You can video him or her doing it, so you'll know how to do it yourself. And remember your tools when you travel—you'll need, at minimum, Allen wrenches, a basic multi-tool, and any specialized items for your particular bike.

A POINT-TO-POINT TOUR

Big bike trips sometimes mean landing in one city and departing from another. Instead of a loop, you're going "point-to-point." In this case, you'll need to assemble your bike and ditch the box it traveled in, so a homemade cardboard job is the best call in this instance. Once you complete your tour and you're ready to head home, you'll need to locate and build another box.

Sounds tricky, but with some friendly, enthusiastic emailing, you'll be surprised what a bike shop in Dublin or Dubai or Durban might do for you. You can also check adventure cycling forums online and post your travel itinerary. Other riders might know a shop or hotel in your departure city that'd be willing to help. Just repay the favor someday, to the folks who helped you or another intrepid traveler you encounter on the road. Bike karma—a powerful force in the universe!

How to Beat the Airlines at Their Own Game— "Breakaway" Bikes

"Breakaway" bikes, or bikes that split in two for travel, have become more popular in the past few years. Two companies, Ritchey and S and S, make coupler systems that are built into a bike's frame, allowing you to split the frame and pack it in a box about eighteen inches deep and as big around as a road wheel. Under current regulations, no airlines charge for a box this size, saving you hundreds in excess luggage fees. Saved cash means way more money for gelato while touring in Italy.

TRAINING?! NOBODY SAID ANYTHING ABOUT TRAINING!

Don't freak out, I'm not talking about 6 am runs and eating raw eggs. But, I do want you to have a blast when you head out touring, so let's make sure you're ready.

The most important thing for a few days of adventure cycling is being comfortable. If you do all the planning in the world, have fantastic weather, and set up a great bike, but then find yourself miserably tired or uncomfortable by the first night—game over. By putting in enough training time beforehand, you should be able to get your body ready for the trip ahead.

Make sure your bike fit falls within the ballpark for saddle height and handlebar position. Let's assume you're set as far as those details go.

The next hurdle in staying comfortable is spending enough time in the saddle that your butt, knees, back, hands, and neck are used to it. Going from no cycling at all to six hours a day is going to stress your body, and you'll end up aching, so if you're planning a really big tour, try to make sure you're riding plenty in the months leading up to your trip.

If you've never ridden for a week straight, perhaps a shorter tour—or scheduling a couple of rest days along the way—is in order. If you're going for the long haul, just increase your mileage in the weeks coming up to your tour. Don't increase it by more than 10 percent a week and your body will have time to adapt and strengthen. Two weeks before your trip, taper off your riding to give yourself time to recover.

TRICKS OF THE TRADE

Bike Forums

Since we're talking about forums, note that many cycling sites these days have reader forums for advice, debating trailers versus panniers, posting trip reports, or anything to do with two wheels. Take advantage of them. There are always enthusiastic, helpful people willing to help you avoid mistakes they've already made.

Check out www.BikePacking.net, www.BicycleTouring101.com, and the Adventure Cycling Association site to get started.

STRETCH, BREATHE, AND SMELL THE ROSES

Any time you're out pedaling, whether it's on a trip or not, don't hesitate to take rest breaks. If you're feeling a little tight in your hamstrings, back, or neck, then stretch for a few minutes, enjoy the view, and relax. Racers out training almost never stop, except to fill bottles. Reformed racers (read: me!) and people riding for fun stop all the time—for coffee breaks, for cookies (recognize a theme here?), to snap photos, to put on sunscreen, or even for a swimming hole. It's a way mellower trip, and it gives the body a little break from the bike.

PROTECT THAT BIKE!

Whatever you do, don't get your bike or your gear stolen. Easier said than done, sure, but a few precautions will help.

First off, try never to lock or leave your bike where you can't see it. If you're going into a restaurant or a supermarket, lock it outside of a window. Hopefully you'll be able to watch it while inside, but even if you can't, a would-be thief will be in plain view of somebody inside, and hopefully he or she will think twice about snatching your ride.

For bike tours, big groups usually bring a thin, metal cable for extended stops. When the whole group pulls over for lunch, ride leaders loop the cable through all the bikes and lock it to a fence or lamp post. While a thief could cut the cable pretty easily, at the very least it prevents somebody from just hopping on a bike and pedaling away. When touring, a cable also allows you to lock your trailer or panniers.

If you have a SAG wagon, then don't skimp on locks—bring a traditional "U" lock, as well as a cable. You can also bring a "cable lock," which is just a steel cable that also has a combination lock built into it. It's actually great to have both—that way you can lock up the frame, wheels, and racks.

If you're going self-supported, then weight becomes an issue. The small "U" locks that messengers use are probably the safest, but they won't let you secure your wheels and other equipment. A short section of steel cable is probably worth the extra ounces because of the extra security it provides.

Safer Still: Getting Your Bike out of Sight

Some cyclists also ride with a tent with a "vestibule." A vestibule is a covered entry area: backpackers leave shoes and wet gear in it, but as a cyclist you can roll your bike into it. Zipping the vestibule shut isn't like locking your bike, but it does get it out of sight and makes it more of a hassle for a thief to get at it. It'll cost you an extra pound or two, and a few bucks, but it's worth it.

Vestibule

You can also ask at campgrounds, restaurants, and parks about storage rooms or fenced areas that you can lock your bike in. Again, anything that puts another layer of hassle and security between you and the thieves is a good idea.

Keep Copies of the Important Stuff

Finally, anytime you leave your bike and gear, always have your ID, cash, credit cards, airline tickets, and passport with you. Having a photocopy of these stashed in your gear is a good idea, too, just in case you lose something or get mugged. This way you'll have all your relevant numbers and information with you, so you can cancel cards and get a passport reissued. I've taken to saving copies of my airline tickets, passport, and health insurance info online that way I can access it anywhere there's a computer.

Finding Your Adventure Inspiration

These writers, and one filmmaker, share some of the coolest bike trips imaginable, so check them out:

The Masked Rider: Cycling in West Africa, by Neil Peart. Peart is the drummer from the band "Rush," and it's cool to read about a rock star living cheap and riding around Africa.

Mud, Sweat, and Gears: A Rowdy Family Adventure Across Canada on Seven Wheels, by Joe "Metal Cowboy" Kurmaskie. Joe somehow figures out how to do an amazing bike journey with his whole family, including kids under ten!

Hey Mom, Can I Ride My Bike Across America?: Five Kids Meet Their Country, by John S. Boettner. Young kids going for it, riding across the United States.

I Made It: Goran Kropp's Incredible Journey to the Top of the World. This film documents Kropp riding from Sweden to Mount Everest, soloing it, and riding back. Epic.

Adventure Cycling: My Own Tour de France

By Bob Long

I took up cycling rather late, after retiring from my professional life as a lawyer, and was immediately drawn into the sport—first as just a way to stay fit, and then over time, as what a friend has termed "my organizing principle of life."

As I worked hard at improving my performance on the bike, it soon became apparent that I was never going to be the speediest guy on the road, because of both my late start into cycling and my large-sized frame: I'm over six feet and built more like a football player than cycling star.

As Tour of Italy winner Andy Hampsten once told me when I asked him about training, "Bob, I don't know how to break this to you, but I don't think there is ever going to be a place for you in the Tour."

But I wasn't deterred. I loved to ride and gradually became faster and found that I had pretty strong endurance. I could go long distances, recover quickly, and do it over again. I worked my way into centuries (hundred-mile rides) and other long events and then started looking for other challenges. What immediately appealed to me was doing multi-day events covering significant mileage. Fortunately, my spouse, Susan, also began to get into cycling and found the prospect of doing long cycling trips appealing.

We started with a week-long tour through southern Oregon the first year and then a ten-day tour in eastern British Columbia the next. Both offered the challenge of riding seventy to eighty miles per day and climbing some significant hills and passes, and both provided miles of beautiful terrain and scenery. We soon concluded that there is no better way to see the countryside and absorb the local flavors and colors than from a bicycle.

I then began to set my sights on even longer rides and greater challenges. In short order, I did a thirty-five-day, 2,600-mile trip up the Continental Divide, from southern New Mexico to Jasper, Alberta, and then last summer, a fifty-day, 4,000-mile trip across North America, from the Olympic Peninsula, in Washington, to Bar Harbor, Maine. Both were lifetime experiences.

As I learned to ride long distances, I also gradually improved my climbing abilities and decided I wanted to do even tougher climbs on the bike. One summer, I toured three weeks around Colorado and climbed most of the best known passes in the Rockies, and I have also done the same thing in the Sierra and Cascades. Having handled those, I decided to undertake some of the famous passes in the Italian and French Alps, like the Stelvio, Passo Gavia, Mortirolo, Mont Ventoux, and Galibier. I am still not the speediest, but I get these climbs done steadily and strongly.

Andy Hampsten is right: There is never going to be a place for me in the Tour, but I have learned to ride the same distances and climb the same vertical as any Tour route provides, and I love doing it as much as any Tour rider out there. And as an added joy for me, so does Susan.

Bob Long is an attorney from Pasadena, California. He has toured throughout Europe and North America, logging mileage in the mountains, across deserts, and up and down the coasts. He's as passionate a cyclist as they come.

12

CONCLUSION & RESOURCES

W e started out with a forged da Vinci drawing, survived a couple of world wars, went shopping for bikes, learned how to fit and fix them, witnessed the invention of the mountain bike and BMX, hung out with messengers and their fixies, tried a race or two, and saved the world with bike commuting before touring around it with a trailer and all our gear. Tired? Yeah, me, too!

You can enjoy the bike a thousand different ways, every day of the week, just about anywhere you live. I hope you've gotten a better sense of what kind of cyclist you might want to be, how to get going, and where you're headed. The only essential ingredient here is the getting going—and just start riding. Within a few months, you'll have a better idea of what you're doing, and then—you're on your way.

CYCLING, THE RIDE FOR LIFE

For most people, team sports like baseball and soccer will fall by the wayside after high school. The cool thing about cycling is that it makes the perfect lifetime sport. It's easy on your joints (unlike soccer and running), you don't need a league or pick-up game to enjoy it (unlike most ball sports), and you can incorporate it into your daily routine.

Need to return some library books? No sweat, just do it during your favorite ride: no driving, you'll be healthier for it, and you just saved some dough, too. You have to get to work, and you want to also squeeze in some exercise? Ride to your place of work. Easy. A few weeks of cycling and you won't remember how you survived without it. It's fun, it feels good, and it makes the world a more livable place.

IT JUST MAKES SENSE

No matter how you get the bike into your life, it just makes sense. There are so many benefits, from keeping you fit to reducing your stress to saving the environment to cutting your gasoline bills.

Cycling is one of the few sports you can enjoy with literally everybody—kids, men, women, your grandfather with a knee replacement, a first-time mountain biker, the women's state BMX champion, folks from farm country, inner-city messengers, bike travelers from who-knows-where, and immigrants from cycling-mad countries like France, Australia, and Germany. It's rare to play pick-up basketball with a fifty-eight-year-old cancer survivor and her son, all in the same game. But with cycling, it happens all the time. It's cool!

Cycling gets you places, introduces you to people, and doesn't really have much of a downside, except for the occasional skinned elbow and the cost of good tires. Man, who would've thought a mountain bike tire could cost seventy-five bucks?! Well, that's way cheaper than car tires, so maybe we're still ahead of the game. In any event, cycling's a blast, and I'm hoping you're already psyched.

JUST DO IT

And that's the best way to get going—just do it. If you're undecided between a road bike and a mountain bike, just choose one and give it a shot. With the internet, selling old gear is a snap, so if after six months you decide a jumping bike is really what you wanted instead of a mountain bike, then sign on to Craigslist and start dealing.

Start cycling and you'll gradually discover what you like, both in terms of gear and terrain.

BEYOND HOLY SPOKES

This was a great place to get started, and I hope it's a fun introduction to many different types of cycling, but as soon as you really want to broaden your horizons, you'll need to get some more detailed information.

Local bike clubs and teams are great resources, especially for aspiring racers. Hit a few of the sites mentioned in the previous chapters, seek out a few of the books, or check out our Resources section, and you'll discover more and more about the sport. A quick internet search and you're bound to find even more.

Cycling has become so popular, even in small towns there are usually a few folks getting on the bike. Wherever you are, find some fellow cyclists, and see what they're up to. If they're not doing the kind of riding you're interested in, chances are they'll be able to point you in the right direction. See you out there!

RESOURCES

Whether you're researching rides, finding races, choosing gears, or getting advice, the internet is probably you're best place to start. In addition to that kind of basic background work, don't hesitate to post on message boards and in online forums to solicit more specific advice from other cyclists.

When dealing with national cycling organizations, it's best to try and consult individual chapters for more specific links to sites related to bicycle fit, advocacy, environmental causes, and maintenance.

Here are a few sites to get you started:

WEBSITES

About.com: Bicycling
Bicycling.about.com
This site can answer most of your basic questions about bicycling, plus it has some great video tutorials.

Adventure Cycling Association
AdventureCycling.org
This organization provides maps, guides, and advice for traveling by bicycle.

Bicycle Industry Jobs
BicycleIndustryJobs.com
Find job listings in every part of the bicycling industry here.

Bicycling
Bicycling.com
This online magazine gives you general information, race coverage, health and training advice, gear reviews, and more.

Bike Packing
BikePacking.net
This website gives you routes, forums, and equipment reviews for overnight trips by bike.

Bike Snob NYC
Bikesnobnyc.blogspot.com
Read the daily thoughts, and sometimes rants, of the Bike Snob.

International Mountain Bicycling Association
IMBA.com
This organization advocates for mountain biking and builds and maintains mountain-biking trails.

The League of American Bicyclists
BikeLeague.org
Originally founded in 1880, this organization promotes bicycling for everyone and advocates for a bike-friendly America.

National Interscholastic Cycling Association
NationalMTB.org
Since 2009 this group has been organizing mountain-biking programs for high school students.

USA Cycling
USACycling.org
USA Cycling supports and promotes competitive cycling. Look here for info on races, stats, and professional cyclists' bios.

Velo News
VeloNews.com
Get information on competitive road, cyclo-cross, and mountain biking from this online magazine. They also have great information on training and nutrition.

BOOKS

Advice

Pruitt, Andrew L. Ed.D. Andy Pruitt's *Complete Medical Guide for Cyclists.* VeloPress, 2006

Friel, Joe. *The Cyclist's Training Bible.* VeloPress, 2009

Watson, Graham. *Graham Watson's Tour de France Travel Guide: The Complete Insider's Guide to the Tour!* VeloPress, 2009

Friel, Joe. *The Mountain Biker's Training Bible.* VeloPress, 2000

Zinn, Lennard. Zinn and the *Art of Mountain Bike Maintenance.* VeloPress, 2010

Zinn, Lennard. *Zinn & the Art of Road Bike Maintenance.* VeloPress, 2009

History

Fitzpatrick, Jim. *The Bicycle in Wartime: An Illustrated History.* Star Hill Studio, 2011

Macy, Sue. *Wheels of Change: How Women Rode the Bicycle to Freedom (With a Few Flat Tires Along the Way).* National Geographic Society, 2011

Bike Culture

Weiss, Eben. *Bike Snob: Systematically and Mercilessly Realigning the World of Cycling.* Chronicle Books, 2010

Weiss, Eben. *The Enlightened Cyclist: Commuter Angst, Dangerous Drivers, and Other Obstacles on the Path to Two-Wheeled Transcendence.* Chronicle Books, 2012

Edwards, Andrew, and Leonard, Max. *Fixed: Global Fixed-Gear Bike Culture.* Laurence King Publishers, 2009

Walker, Amy. *On Bicycles: 50 Ways the New Bike Culture Can Change Your Life.* New World Library, 2011

Bicycling Stories

Barry, Michael. *Inside the Bus: My Ride with Lance Armstrong and the U.S. Postal CyclingTeam.* VeloPress, 2005
A fun, inside look at riding with one of the world's best Tour de France teams, alongside the controversial Lance Armstrong.

Boettner, John Seigel. *Hey Mom, Can I Ride My Bike Across America?: Five Kids Meet Their Country.* Sbf Productions, 2000
Young kids going for it, riding across the United States.

Pearl, Neil. *The Masked Rider: Cycling in West Africa.* ECW Press, 2004
Peart is the drummer for the band Rush, and it's cool to read about a rock star living cheap and riding around Africa.

Savage, Barbara. *Miles from Nowhere: A Round the World Bicycle Adventure.* Mountaineers Books, 1985
Brave, engaging, and inspiring, Barbara Savage and her partner hit the road.

Kurmaskie, Joe. *Mud, Sweat, and Gears: A Rowdy Family Adventure Across Canada on Seven Wheels.* Breakaway Books, 2011
Joe somehow figures out how to do an amazing bike journey with his whole family, including kids under ten!

Krabbe, Tim. *The Rider.* Bloomsbury USA, 2003
The fictional tale of one rider's experience in a grueling, tough race.

FILMS

American Flyers
This film about two brothers making it in professional road racing stars a young Kevin Costner.

I Made It: Goran Kropp's Incredible Journey to the Top of the World
This film documents Kropp riding from Sweden to Mount Everest, soloing it, and riding back. Epic.

Kranked REVOLVE
You'll see mind-blowing footage of mountain biking in Vancouver and beyond in this film.

Seasons
The film follows professional freeriders, downhillers, and racers through four seasons, giving you a glimpse of what it's like to live the biking life.

WATCH ONLINE

Danny MacAskill
Dannymacaskill.co.uk
Click on "Videos" and watch the master in action.

New World Disorder
Nwdfilms.com/
These guys make amazing mountain-biking videos.

The 1989 Tour de France
Watch Greg LeMond's miraculous eight-second victory.

The 1989 World Cycling Championships
See Greg LeMond's spectacular win over Irishman Sean Kelly.

ABOUT THE AUTHOR

A BMX hellion as a kid and a road racer into his 20s, today Rob Coppolillo acts as a guide on bike trips in Italy and on mountain bike expeditions anywhere it's pretty. He makes literally tens of hundreds of dollars annually as a writer for *VeloNews, Rocky Mountain Sports,* and *Climbing,* and lives in Boulder, Colorado, with his wife, Rebel, and their twins, Luca and Dominic.

ACKNOWLEDGMENT

I'd like to thank Daniel Harmon, Hallie Warshaw, and all of the crew at Zest Books for their advice, help, and guidance. An especially big thanks to Alec Dinner, a great friend and my unpaid agent—you've kept me afloat, professionally and personally, for two decades and counting. To Sports and Fitness Publishing and the old-school posse at *VeloNews* for publishing my first rough attempts at journalism and getting me going in the world—much appreciated!

Most of all, to a funky, fun, and fantastic cast of characters, many of whom I met through cycling—Jordan Kobert, Pete Isert, Jimmy Mo, Chris Wherry, Andy Hampsten, Chuck Ibis, Scot Nicol, Phil Voorhees, Jonny Coln, Bobby Soderstrom, Andy Farrand, Ashley McCullough, Jimmy Mac, Rick Lofaro, Luca Boscardin, Chris Grealish, Mark Mahan, Enrico Caracciolo, Jeremy Gage, and all of you I'm forgetting. Thanks for the encouragement, couches on which to crash, and good times. Love you all.

MORE FROM ZEST BOOKS!

47 Things You Can Do for the Environment
by Lexi Petronis with environmental consultant Jill Buck

97 Things You Should Do Before You Finish High School
by Erika Stalder

Crap
How to Deal with Annoying Teachers, Bosses, Backstabbers,
and Other Stuff that Stinks

By Erin Elisabeth Conley, Karen Macklin, and Jake Miller

Dead Strange
The Bizarre Truths Behind 50 Unexplained Mysteries

By Matt Lamy

Don't Sit on the Baby
The Ultimate Guide to Sane, Skilled, and Safe Babysitting

By Halley Bondy

The End
50 Apocalyptic Visions From Pop Culture
That You Should Know About…Before It's too Late

by Laura Barcella

The How-To Handbook
Tips, Tricks, Shortcuts, and Solutions for the Problems of Everyday Life

By Martin Oliver and Alexandra Johnson

How to Fight, Lie, and Cry Your Way to Popularity and a Prom Date
Lousy Life Lessons from 50 Teen Movies

By Nikki Roddy

In the Driver's Seat
A Girl's Guide to Her First Car

By Erika Stalder

Reel Culture
50 Classic Movies You Should Know About
(So You Can Impress Your Friends)

by Mimi O'Connor

Scandalous!
50 Shocking Events You Should Know About
(So You Can Impress Your Friends)

by Hallie Fryd

Start It Up
The Complete Teen Business Guide to Turning Your Passions Into Pay

By Kenrya Rankin

Super-Pop
Pop Culture Lists to Help You Win at Trivia, Survive in the
Wild, and Make It Through the Holidays

By Daniel Harmon

Where's My Stuff?
The Ultimate Teen Organizing Guide

By Samantha Moss with Teen Organizer Lesley Schwartz